David Henry Hwang is an acclaimed playwright, screenwriter,
and librettist. He won the 1988 Tony Award for *M. Butterfly*.
His many honors include the PEN/Laura Pels Award for Master
American Dramatist and the Steinberg Distinguished Playwright
Award. He currently serves as chair of the American Theatre
Wing, writes and produces for Showtime's *The Affair*, and heads
the playwriting program at Columbia University School of the
Arts.

M. BUTTERFLY

BROADWAY TIE-IN EDITION

With a New Introduction by the Playwright

DAVID HENRY HWANG

PLUME BOOKS

PLUME
An imprint of Penguin Random House LLC
375 Hudson Street
New York, New York 10014

M. Butterfly was previously published, in its entirety,
in *American Theatre* magazine, and also in Plume paperback.

REGISTERED TRADEMARK—MARCA REGISTRADA

Library of Congress Cataloging-in-Publication Data
has been applied for.

ISBN 9780525533719 (Broadway Tie-in Edition)

Printed in the United States of America

THE FURTHER METAMORPHOSIS
OF A BUTTERFLY

I realize this is a bit unusual. As a playwright, I've had the extreme good fortune of enjoying a career that has lasted almost four decades so far. Yet even after all this time, *M. Butterfly*, a play I wrote when I was twenty-eight, remains the work for which I'm best known. It's rather more common for an author, later in life, to rewrite a piece that was deemed unsuccessful in its original incarnation. So why am I choosing to rework arguably my most renowned play?

I can offer two reasons, each of which alone would seem to me insufficient explanation. First, I have learned so much more since the original Broadway production in 1988 about the true story on which this play is based. I first encountered news of a scandalous espionage trial involving a French diplomat stationed in Beijing and his lover of twenty years, a Chinese opera performer, as a one-column item buried in the back pages of *The New York Times*. In those pre-Internet days, it wasn't easy to gain access to newspapers from abroad. Stuart Ostrow, who eventually produced the show on Broadway, assisted me with some early funding for research, but the few articles I found didn't shed much more light on the actual story. So I went ahead and wrote the play anyway, using the bare facts of the real-life trial as a jumping-off point for my own imagination. Actually, that worked out very well. I even invented some story points that turned out to be true—for instance, that the real diplomat, Bernard Boursicot, tried to commit suicide in prison.

In the wake of *M. Butterfly*'s Broadway success, however, much more came out about the actual case. Back in the eighties, news organizations still had the resources to send reporters abroad to pursue interesting stories. So *People* magazine profiled the real-life models for my characters Gallimard and Song. Barbara Walters went to Paris to interview them. At the time, the real story felt to me ironically like a footnote to my play—yet, even then, undeniably fascinating.

By the mid-2010s, however, as we began to consider reviving *M. Butterfly* on Broadway, the way we think about gender fluidity had also changed considerably since the play's premiere. Again, this in and of itself would not be sufficient reason to consider rewriting the piece. But I began to remember the details of the true story, so interesting even in the afterglow of the show's initial success. These facts suggested a more nuanced, less gender-binary version of the story.

These two factors—greater knowledge of the true story and an awareness that our world had thankfully moved forward towards a more complicated understanding of gender identity and fluidity—combined to make me want to revisit this material anew. One of the things that makes me proud about the original play is that it arguably anticipated "intersectionality": the notion that race, gender, and sexual identity are linked, that it's not possible to truly address one type of stereotyping without considering them all. In that same spirit, I decided to take the leap and brave reconsidering the story of the French diplomat and the Chinese opera singer.

As of the writing of this introduction, we are more than a month away from the opening night of this Broadway revival of *M. Butterfly*. I have no idea whether this new version will come to be judged a success or a disappointment. So there is a certain purity in wanting at this moment to thank director Julie Taymor for her guidance and inspiration, as well as our courageous lead producer, Nelle Nugent. Whatever the fate of this revision, I'm continuing to do what I've done throughout my career: take risks, try to tell the truth, and make the best show I can. Then we leave its fate to the theatre gods.

David Henry Hwang

Brooklyn, New York
September 2017

M. Butterfly, presented by Stuart Ostrow and David Geffen, and directed by John Dexter, premiered on February 10, 1988, at the National Theatre in Washington, D.C., and opened on Broadway March 20, 1988, at the Eugene O'Neill Theatre. *M. Butterfly* won the 1988 Tony for best play, the Outer Critics Circle Award for best Broadway play, the John Gassner Award for best American play, and the Drama Desk Award for best new play. It had the following cast:

Kurogo	Alec Mapa, Chris Odo, Jamie H. J. Guan
Rene Gallimard	John Lithgow
Song Liling	B. D. Wong
Marc/Man #2/Consul Sharpless	John Getz
Renee/Woman at Party/Girl in Magazine	Lindsay Frost
Comrade Chin/Suzuki/Shu Fang	Lori Tan Chinn
Helga	Rose Gregorio
M. Toulon/Man #1/Judge	George N. Martin

Scenery and Costumes: Eiko Ishioka
Lighting: Andy Phillips
Hair: Phyllis Della
Music: Giacomo Puccini, Lucia Hwong
Casting: Meg Simon, Fran Kumin
Production Stage Manager: Bob Borod
Peking Opera Consultants: Jamie H. J. Guan & Michelle Ehlers
Musical Director and Lute: Lucia Hwong
Percussion, Shakuhachi, and Guitar: Yukio Tsuji
Violin and Percussion: Jason Hwang
Musical Coordinator: John Miller

The Broadway revival opened on October 26, 2017, at the Cort Theatre, with the following cast.

Rene Gallimard	Clive Owen
Song Liling	Jin Ha
Renee/Pinup Girl/Others	Clea Alsip
Marc/Pinkerton/Others	Murray Bartlett
Toulon/Sharpless/Judge/Others	Michael Countryman
Comrade Chin/Others	Celeste Den
Agnes/Others	Enid Graham
Dancers	Emmanuel Brown, Jess Fry, Jason Garcia Ignacio, Kristin Faith Oei, Scott Weber, Erica Wong

Directed by Julie Taymor
Original Music by Elliot Goldenthal
Choreography by Ma Cong
Scenic Design by Paul Steinberg
Costume Design by Constance Hoffman
Lighting Design by Donald Holder
Sound Design by Will Pickens
Percussion and Accordion by Jianpeng Feng
Wig and Hair Design by Dave Bova
Makeup Design by Judy Chin
Production Stage Managing by Robert Bennett
Casting by Telsey + Company/Will Cantler, CSA, & Adam Caldwell, CSA

M. BUTTERFLY is produced by Nelle Nugent, Steve Traxler, Kenneth Teaton, Benjamin Feldman, Doug Morris, Suzanne Gilad and Larry Rogowsky, Jim Kierstead, Hunter Arnold, Spencer Ross, Jam Theatricals, and in association with Alix L. Ritchie, Kades-Reese, Storyboard Entertainment, and Jeffrey Sosnick.

PLAYWRIGHT'S NOTES

A former French diplomat and a Chinese opera singer have been sentenced to six years in jail for spying for China after a two-day trial that traced a story of clandestine love and mistaken sexual identity. . . . Mr. Bouriscot was accused of passing information to China after he fell in love with Mr. Shi, whom he believed for twenty years to be a woman.
　　　　　　　—*The New York Times*, May 11, 1986

This play was suggested by international newspaper accounts of a recent espionage trial. For purposes of dramatization, names have been changed, characters created, and incidents devised or altered, and this play does not purport to be a factual record of real events or real people.

> I could escape this feeling
> With my China girl . . .
> —David Bowie & Iggy Pop

SETTING

The action of the play takes place in a Paris prison in 1986, and in recall, the 1950s in France, the 1960s and 1970s in China, and the 1970s and 1980s in Paris.

ACT ONE

SCENE 1

Gallimard's prison cell. Paris. 1986.

Lights fade up to reveal RENE GALLIMARD, 40s.

GALLIMARD: Butterfly, Butterfly . . .

> *(He speaks to us)*

I am confined to this cell day and night. And yet, I've found prison to be something of a refuge. This is no doubt due to the fact that I'm not an ordinary prisoner. You see, I'm a celebrity.

> *(Pause)*

I never dreamed this day would arrive. I've never been considered witty or clever. In fact, as a young boy, in an informal poll among my grammar school classmates, I was voted "least likely to be invited to a party." It's a title I managed to hold on to for many years. Despite some stiff competition.

> *(Pause)*

But now, how the tables turn! Look at me: the life of every social function in Paris. Paris? Why be modest? My fame has spread to London, Tokyo, New York. Listen to them! In the world's smartest parties. I'm the one who lifts their spirits!

With a flourish, Gallimard directs our
attention to another part of the stage.

SCENE 2

A party. 1986.

Well-dressed MEN and WOMEN make conversation.
Gallimard observes them from his cell.

WOMAN 1: And what of Gallimard?

MAN 1: Gallimard?

WOMAN 2, MAN 2, AND WOMAN 3: Gallimard!

WOMAN 1: He still claims not to believe the truth.

WOMAN 2: What?

MAN 1: Still?

MAN 2: Even since the trial?

WOMAN 1: Yes. Isn't it mad?

MAN 1:

(*Laughing*)

He says . . .

MAN 1 AND WOMAN 3: . . . it was dark . . .

MAN 1 AND WOMAN 1: . . . and she was very modest!

MAN 2: So—what? He never touched her with his hands?

WOMAN 1: Perhaps he did, and simply misidentified the equipment.

WOMAN 2: A compelling case for sex education in the schools.

WOMAN 3: To protect the national security!

MAN 1: Church can't argue with that.

MAN 2: That's impossible!

ALL: How could he not know?

MAN 1: Simple ignorance.

MAN 2: For twenty years?

WOMAN 2: Time flies when you're being stupid.

WOMAN 3: Well, I thought the French were ladies' men.

WOMAN 1: It seems Monsieur Gallimard was overly anxious to live up to his national reputation.

MAN 2: Instead, he's become a national embarrassment.

WOMAN 2: A laughingstock.

MAN 1 AND MAN 2 : A fool.

WOMAN 3: Actually, I feel sorry for him.

WOMAN 1: A toast! To Monsieur Gallimard!

WOMAN 2 AND WOMAN 3: Yes! To Gallimard!

ALL: To Gallimard!

MAN 1: Vive la différence!

> *They toast, laughing. Lights down on them.*

SCENE 3

Gallimard's cell.

GALLIMARD: You see? They toast me. I've become patron saint of the socially inept. Can they really be so foolish? Men like that—they should be scratching at my door, begging to learn my secrets! For I, Rene Gallimard, you see, I have known, and been loved by . . . the Perfect Woman.

> *(Pause)*

Alone in this cell, I sit night after night, watching our story play through my head, always searching for a new ending, one that redeems my honor, where she returns at last to my arms. And I imagine you—my ideal audience—who come to understand and even, perhaps just a little, to envy me.

> *(Over the house speakers, we hear the opening
> phrases of* Madame Butterfly)

In order for you to understand what I did and why, I must introduce you to my favorite opera: *Madama Butterfly*. By Giacomo Puccini. First produced at La Scala, Milan, in 1904, it is now beloved throughout the Western world.

(Pause)

(GALLIMARD CONT.): And why not? Its heroine, Cio-Cio-San, also known as Butterfly, is a feminine ideal, beautiful and brave. My parents took me to the opera only once—as a boy of twelve. I got all dressed up as if for Christmas Mass—and headed into the city to our provincial opera house. A crystal chandelier hung from the ceiling, and a man in a velvet uniform showed us to our plush red seats. Then the room got very quiet, and all the lights went dark. As the curtain rose, I saw . . .

> *(PINKERTON [played by the actor who will portray MARC], an American naval officer, enters)*

Lieutenant Benjamin Franklin Pinkerton of the U.S. Navy.

> *(Pinkerton lip-syncs over a recording of the "Dovunque al mondo" aria from the opera)*

The tenor in his sailor suit sang with such power and beauty. Sweeping my heart towards far-off lands—where a man who loved adventure finds himself with all the world—and a beautiful girl—at his feet. At the time, I barely understood the story. All I really heard—and felt—was the music. So grand and majestic that it carried me away.

> *(SHARPLESS [played by the actor who will portray TOULON] enters)*

PINKERTON: Consul!

GALLIMARD: The Honorable Sharpless, United States Consul to Japan.

PINKERTON: Milk, punch, or whiskey?

GALLIMARD: Over the years, I came to understand what they're actually singing.

SHARPLESS: Whiskey. So what's her name?

PINKERTON: Cio-Cio-San. Her friends call her Butterfly. I'm marrying her in Japanese fashion: for 999 years.

SHARPLESS: That's honorable.

PINKERTON: With the right to cancel my contract every month!

SHARPLESS: That's not so honorable.

PINKERTON: And you know how much she cost?

SHARPLESS: Pinkerton! You're not buying her!

PINKERTON: True, it's more like a rental. A hundred yen! That's—what?—a dollar?

SHARPLESS: Is there any chance—you love her?

PINKERTON: I'm really excited, does that count?

SHARPLESS: So you're going to break her heart.

PINKERTON: I must have her, pin those delicate wings with my needle, even if they break. America forever!

> *The American national anthem theme from* Madame Butterfly *creeps in over the speakers. Pinkerton and Sharpless lip-sync their duet, then exit.*

GALLIMARD: Today, of course, I realize that women who put their total worth at roughly one American dollar are quite hard to find. But when I was a boy, the closest we came was in the pages of girlie magazines. I first discovered them at age ten. In my uncle's house. In his closet—all lined up—my body shook. Here were women—a shelfful—who would do exactly what I wanted.

> *The "Love Duet" creeps in over the speakers.*
> *The upstage special area reveals a PINUP GIRL*
> *(the actress who will later play RENEE) in a sexy*
> *negligee.*

PINUP GIRL: I know you're watching me.

GALLIMARD: My throat . . . it's dry.

PINUP GIRL: You want to see, don't you?

GALLIMARD: Yes. I want to see.

PINUP GIRL: Of course you do. Want make to take these off? These flimsy little things?

GALLIMARD: Yeah, take them off!

PINUP GIRL: Oh, you are bad.

GALLIMARD: Yes, I am bad. I'm going to look at you—

PINUP GIRL: So you might as well see—

GALLIMARD: Whether you like it or—

PINUP GIRL: —everything.

GALLIMARD: Oh.

Pinup Girl: All of me.

Gallimard: Oh my god.

Pinup Girl: It's what you want, right?

Gallimard: Huh?

Pinup Girl: Nothing left to the imagination.

Gallimard: Yeah, that's what I want.

Pinup Girl: I want that too.

Gallimard: You do?

Pinup Girl: To show myself to you—without shame.

Gallimard: I—wouldn't have guessed that.

Pinup Girl: So what are *you* going to do?

Gallimard: What?

Pinup Girl: Now that you've got me, where you want me?

Gallimard: That's right.

Pinup Girl: So?

Gallimard: I've got you.

Pinup Girl: So do it.

Gallimard: I will!

Pinup Girl: Do it now.

Gallimard: Wait, I just . . .

PINUP GIRL: What's wrong?

GALLIMARD: Nothing! I just need a little more . . . time.

PINUP GIRL: Guess you're not so bad after all.

>   *Blackout on Pinup Girl.*

GALLIMARD:

>   *(To us)*

I closed the magazines. Put them back up on the shelves. And never went into my uncle's closet again. But on that night, at the opera, my body shook once more—with the entrance of Butterfly.

>   *(Music from the opera plays on the house speakers, accompanying a display of* Japonaise. *Perhaps we see Butterfly's shadow)*

As she glides past, beautiful, laughing softly behind her fan, I found myself sighing with hope. Even the son of a butcher could dare to believe, like Pinkerton, that I deserved a Butterfly. She arrives with all her possessions in the folds of her sleeves, lays them all out, for her man to do with as he pleases. Even her life itself—she bows her head as she whispers that she's not even worth the hundred yen he paid for her. He's already given too much, when we know he's really had to give nothing at all.

SCENE 4

École Nationale. Aix-en-Provence. 1955.

MARC enters.

MARC: Oh god, turn that blasted wailing down!

Music out.

GALLIMARD: Sorry, Marc, I was just—

MARC: Aren't you coming with us?

GALLIMARD: I can't. I'm writing a paper on Commodore Perry's expedition to Japan, and—

MARC: That can wait! We are going to Dad's villa in Marseille! You know what happened last time?

GALLIMARD: Of course I do!

MARC: Of course you don't! You never know.... They stripped, Rene!

GALLIMARD: Who stripped?

MARC: The girls!

GALLIMARD: Girls? Who said anything about girls?

MARC: Rene, we are a buncha university guys goin' to the beach. What are we gonna do—talk philosophy?

GALLIMARD: What girls? Where do you get them?

MARC: Who cares? Word gets around. Anyway, they come. Wave after wave of hot little lemmings. Crashing up onto our shore.

GALLIMARD: You mean, they just—?

MARC: Before you know it, every last one of them—they're splashing in the water. When the moon reflects off the ocean, you can see just enough—not too much—smooth young flesh, jiggling boobs, tight round asses; just enough, to make them all—perfect. You reach out and whatever you grab—will not disappoint. You're in there, going at it, on and on for as long as you can stand. Feeling like a god.

GALLIMARD: What happens in the morning?

MARC: In the morning, you're ready to talk some philosophy.

GALLIMARD: With the girls?

MARC: Huh? No, they're gone by then. That's the beauty part! It's perfect for a guy like you, really.

GALLIMARD: What do you mean by that?

MARC: You seem to develop a speech impediment every time you come face-to-face with a pair of boobs.

GALLIMARD: I just—I don't wanna say anything wrong.

MARC: Great, see? They don't even have to say yes.

GALLIMARD: But what about—the wine? Dinner? Candlelight?

MARC: Oh my god. Moonlight's not good enough for you? Look, you're always gonna stay a virgin—

GALLIMARD: I'm not a virgin!

MARC: —until you learn to take what you want. I mean, you're not even bad-looking. So how 'bout it?

GALLIMARD: Maybe next time.

MARC: Fucking hopeless.

> *Marc walks over to the other side of the stage and starts waving and smiling at women in the audience.*

GALLIMARD:

> *(To us)*

We now return to my version of *Madame Butterfly* and the events leading to my recent conviction for treason.

> *(Gallimard notices Marc making lewd gestures at the audience)*

Marc, what are you doing?

MARC: Rene, there're a lot of great babes out there. They're no doubt looking at me and thinking, "Ah! A sophisticated Frenchman."

GALLIMARD: This is my story, not yours.

MARC: More's the pity.

> *(To audience)*

À tout à l'heure.

> *Marc exits, leering.*

SCENE 5

Gallimard's cell.

GALLIMARD: In Act Two, Pinkerton's returned to America, and Butterfly has given birth to their child. Three years she has faithfully waited for him to return, even turning down a marriage proposal from a Japanese prince. Finally, she spots in the harbor an American ship—the *Abramo Lincoln*!

> *(Music cue: "Flower Duet")*

This is the moment that redeems her years of waiting.

> *AGNES enters.*

AGNES: Aren't you ready yet, dear? I'm running late.

> *She helps him change into his tuxedo.*

GALLIMARD: You're not coming with me tonight?

AGNES: I have the wives' meeting! It's very important for me to establish myself on the female circuit, you know. I'm actually becoming quite good at *mah jongg*.

GALLIMARD:

> *(To us)*

I married a woman older than myself—Agnes.

AGNES:

> *(To us)*

AGNES (CONT.): I grew up in Australia, among criminals and kangaroos. My father was ambassador there.

GALLIMARD: Hearing that brought me to the altar—

> (Agnes exits)

—where I opted for a dose of practicality. An unsophisticated boy from a provincial town could still manage a quick leap up the career ladder. She may not be my fantasy woman, but she could help me reach the far-off lands of my dreams.

> (Pause)

I married at age twenty-two. I was faithful to my marriage for five years. But practicality had long since lost its charm by the time we arrived in China. The truth is, I yearned to feel more.

> (SONG enters—dressed as Cio-Cio-San)

And so that night, as a junior-level diplomat in puritanical Peking, in a parlor at the Swiss ambassador's house, during the Reign of a Hundred Flowers, I first saw her . . . singing the death scene from *Madame Butterfly*.

SCENE 6

Swiss ambassador's house. Beijing. 1964.

The upstage special area now becomes a stage. Several chairs face upstage, representing a parlor. A few "diplomats"

*in formal dress enter and take seats. Orchestral
accompaniment on the tape is now replaced by a simple
piano. Song performs the death scene from the point where
Butterfly uncovers the hara-kiri knife.*

GALLIMARD: The ending is devastating. Pinkerton sends his
American wife to pick up Butterfly's child. The truth, long
deferred, has come to her door.

> *Song, playing Butterfly, sings the lines from the
> opera in her own voice—which, though not
> classical, should be decent.*

SONG: "Con onor muore / chi non può serbar / vita con onore."

GALLIMARD:

> *(Simultaneously)*

"Death with honor / Is better than life / Life with dishonor."

> *(Song proceeds to play out an abbreviated
> death scene. Everyone in the room applauds. Song
> takes her bows. Others in the room rush to
> congratulate her. Gallimard remains with us)*

They say in opera the voice is everything. Yet here—here was a
Butterfly with little or no voice—but she had the grace, the
delicacy. I believed this girl. I believed her suffering. I
wanted to take her in my arms—so delicate, even I could
protect her, take her home, pamper her, ease her pain.

> *Over the course of the preceding speech, Song
> has broken from the upstage crowd and moved
> towards Gallimard.*

Song: Excuse me. Monsieur . . . ?

Gallimard: Oh! Gallimard. Mademoiselle . . . ?

Song: "Mademoiselle"? How charming. Song Liling.

Gallimard: A beautiful performance.

Song: Oh, please.

Gallimard: I usually—

Song: You embarrass me. I'm no opera singer at all.

Gallimard: I'm so often disappointed by *Butterfly*.

Song: I can't blame you in the least.

Gallimard: I mean, the story—

Song: Ridiculous.

Gallimard: I like the story, but . . . what?

Song: Oh, you like it?

Gallimard: I . . . what I mean is, I usually see it played by huge women in so much bad makeup.

Song: Bad makeup is not unique to the West.

Gallimard: But who can believe them?

Song: And you believe me?

Gallimard: Absolutely. You were utterly convincing. It's the first time—

SONG: Convincing? As a Japanese woman? The Japanese used hundreds of our people for medical experiments during the war, you know. But I gather such an irony is lost on you.

GALLIMARD: No! I was about to say, it's the first time I've seen the beauty of the story.

SONG: Really?

GALLIMARD: Of her death. It's a . . . a pure sacrifice. He's unworthy, but what can she do? She loves him . . . so much. It's a very beautiful story.

SONG: Well, yes, to a Westerner.

GALLIMARD: Excuse me?

SONG: It's one of your favorite fantasies, isn't it? The submissive Oriental woman and the cruel white man.

GALLIMARD: Well, I didn't quite mean . . .

SONG: Consider it this way: What would you say if a blond homecoming queen fell in love with a short Japanese businessman? He treats her cruelly, then goes home for three years, during which time she prays to his picture and turns down marriage from a young Kennedy. Then, when she learns he has remarried, she kills herself. Now, I believe you would consider this girl to be a deranged idiot, correct? But because it's an Oriental who kills herself for a Westerner— ah!—you find it beautiful.

Silence.

GALLIMARD: Yes . . . well . . . I see your point . . .

Song: I will never do this Butterfly again, Monsieur Gallimard. If you wish to see the true Butterfly story, come to the Peking Opera sometime. Expand your mind.

> *Song walks offstage.*

Gallimard:

> *(To us)*

So much for protecting her in my big Western arms.

SCENE 7

> *Gallimard's apartment. Beijing. 1964.*

> *Gallimard changes from his tux into a casual suit. Agnes enters.*

Gallimard: The Chinese are an incredibly arrogant people.

Agnes: They warned us about that in Paris, remember?

Gallimard: Even Parisians consider them arrogant. That's a switch.

Agnes: What is it that Madame Su says? "We are a very old civilization." I never know if she's talking about her country or herself.

Gallimard: I walk around here, all I hear every day, everywhere, is how old this culture is. The fact that "old" may be synonymous with "senile" doesn't occur to them.

AGNES: You're not going to change them. "East is East, West is West, and . . ." whatever that fellow said.

GALLIMARD: It's just that—silly. I met . . . at Ambassador Good-paster's tonight—you should've been there.

AGNES: Goodpaster? Oh god, no. Did he enchant you all again with the history of the cuckoo clock?

GALLIMARD: No. I met, I suppose, the Chinese equivalent of a diva. She's a singer in the Chinese opera.

AGNES: They have an opera, too? Do they sing in Chinese? Or maybe—in Italian?

GALLIMARD: Tonight, she did sing in Italian.

AGNES: How'd she manage that?

GALLIMARD: She must've been educated before the revolution. Her French is very good also. Anyway, she sang the death scene from *Madame Butterfly*.

AGNES: *Madame Butterfly*! Then I should have come. Did she have a nice costume? I think it's a classic piece of music.

GALLIMARD: That's what *I* thought, too. Don't let her hear you say that.

AGNES: What's wrong?

GALLIMARD: Evidently the Chinese hate it.

AGNES: She hated it, but she performed it anyway? Is she per-verse?

GALLIMARD: They hate it because the white man gets the girl. Sour grapes if you ask me.

AGNES: Politics again? Why can't they just hear it as a piece of beautiful music? So, what's in their opera?

GALLIMARD: I don't know. But, whatever it is, I'm sure it must be *old*.

    Agnes exits.

SCENE 8

Chinese opera house and the streets of Beijing.

GALLIMARD: My wife's innocent question kept ringing in my ears. I asked around, but no one knew anything about the Chinese opera. Finally, my curiosity overcame my cowardice. This Chinese diva—this unwilling Butterfly—what did she do to make her so proud?

    (Pause)

The room was hot, and full of smoke. Wrinkled faces, old women, teeth missing—a man with a growth on his neck, like a human toad. All smiling, pipes falling from their mouths, cracking nuts between their teeth, a live chicken pecking at my foot. But all that chaos and clatter faded away in an instant—when I watched her float onto the stage.

    The upstage area is suddenly hit with a harsh
    white light. It is a stage. Accompanied by four
    dancers, Song performs a scene from the Chinese

opera The Butterfly Lovers. *Then drums suddenly slam to a halt. Song strikes a pose, looking straight at Gallimard. Light change. Song walks off the stage and up to Gallimard.*

SONG: Yes. You. White man. I'm looking straight at you.

GALLIMARD: Me?

SONG: You see any other white men? It was too easy to spot you. How often does a man in my audience come in a tie?

Now they are backstage, and the show is over. Gallimard watches as Song changes out of her costume, emerging from behind a screen in an androgynous Mao suit. Gender ambiguous, Song now looks like a beautiful man.

SONG: So, you are an adventurous imperialist?

GALLIMARD: I . . . thought it would further my education.

SONG: It took you four weeks. Why?

GALLIMARD: I've been busy.

SONG: Well, education has always been undervalued in the West, hasn't it?

GALLIMARD: I don't think it's true.

SONG: No, you wouldn't. You're a Westerner. How can you objectively judge your own values?

GALLIMARD: I think it's possible to achieve some distance.

SONG: Do you? Did you enjoy my Butterfly story?

GALLIMARD: Well, it takes a bit of—I mean, to the Western ear—

SONG: It is an acquired taste, perhaps. Which you have now begun to acquire. This opera is called *The Butterfly Lovers*.

GALLIMARD: And the story was rather difficult to—

SONG: My character is a girl. Who, in order to be educated, disguises herself as a boy. I fall in love with another classmate—also male, of course. He finds he has feelings for me—which he cannot understand. Finally, I can hold the truth inside me no longer. It bursts forth—too late. I've already been betrothed to a wealthy merchant, and my true love—dies of heartbreak. On the way to my wedding, I throw myself into his grave. But heaven takes mercy on us. We two are reborn—as butterflies, to be together forever.

(*Pause*)

Now, isn't that more beautiful than your Cio-Cio-San?

GALLIMARD: They're both tragic love stories—

SONG: But in mine, the girl and the boy love as equals.

(*Pause*)

It stinks in here. Let's go.

GALLIMARD: These are the smells of your loyal fans.

SONG: I love them for being my fans. I hate the smell they leave behind. I, too, can distance myself from my people.

(*Looks around, then whispers in his ear*)

"Art for the masses" is a shitty excuse to keep artists poor. Come.

(They move out into the streets)

SONG (CONT.): How I wish there was even one nightclub still open in this city. With martinis, and men in tuxedos, and bad expatriate jazz.

GALLIMARD: If my history serves me correctly, Chinese were not even allowed into clubs before the revolution.

SONG: Not entirely. True, there were signs reading, "No dogs and Chinamen." But women—delicate Chinese women—always went where they pleased. Could you imagine it otherwise? Clubs in Shanghai filled with pasty white women, while hundreds of slender lotus blossoms waited just outside the door? The clubs would be empty. Chinese girls have always held a certain fascination for Caucasian men, isn't that true?

GALLIMARD: I've—never really thought much about it before.

SONG: Well, now that you're in China, perhaps you will.

GALLIMARD: Honestly, in these Mao suits—it's hard to tell the men from the women.

SONG: True. And so sad. They've taken all the beauty from our world. At least we still have the opera.

GALLIMARD: And in your opera, men play women's roles?

SONG: This is changing, but in my form, the Yunnan Opera, we still prefer the traditional way. Which I think is best. But a woman playing a man—*that* I would find interesting. Oh—this is my flat.

GALLIMARD: I didn't even—

SONG: Thank you. Come again next Thursday, and we will further expand your mind.

Song exits. Gallimard turns back to us.

GALLIMARD: What was that? We spoke so easily, without the awkwardness I usually feel around women. Seems I was mistaken. About Monsieur Song. So I've made a friend. This is all for the best. After all, I'm a married man.

SCENE 9

Gallimard's bedroom.

Agnes enters.

AGNES: You didn't tell me you'd be home late.

GALLIMARD: It wasn't my intention. Something came up.

AGNES: Like what?

GALLIMARD: We went to the home of the ambassador from Liechtenstein. You know, they've had an embassy here since the 1950s.

AGNES: And that's why you went? Out of historical curiosity?

GALLIMARD: No, you know how it is. You're sharing a drink with the boys from the office, and then—

AGNES: Someone says, "I've been thinking about Liechtenstein."

GALLIMARD: No, he—the ambassador—he invited us. Of course.

AGNES: Of course.

>   *(Pause)*

Well, I had a good night too. I went with the ladies to a martial arts demonstration. Some of those men—when they break those thick boards—

>   *(She fans herself)*

Whoo-hoo!

>   *Agnes exits. Lights dim.*

GALLIMARD: I lied to my wife. Why? I've never had any reason to lie before. But what reason did I have tonight? I didn't do anything wrong.

>   *(Upstage, Song enters, performing as Madame*
>   *White Snake, from the opera of the same name)*

When I returned to the opera the following week, I saw Song Liling in a very different role.

>   *(Song and the dancers fight in a martial arts*
>   *battle sequence)*

Amidst the ocean of strange faces, I felt the presence of a spectator much more familiar. An angel? Spirit? No—my friend Marc, from school.

>   *Marc enters, as fight scene continues upstage.*

MARC: Rene! You still need me.

GALLIMARD: What are you doing here?

MARC: Looking out for you, as usual. Look, I even brought snacks.

> *Marc hands Gallimard a bag of gummy bear–type sour candies.*

GALLIMARD: Oh, thank you.

MARC: I wasn't going to let you munch on chicken feet, now, was I?

> *They eat the snacks as they watch the opera.*

MARC: Why are you here? Because the music is so beautiful? I've heard cats copulating with greater artistry.

GALLIMARD: The battle is quite exciting.

MARC: Rene: You made a mistake! It's time to cut your losses.

GALLIMARD: A mistake?

MARC: I admire your ambition. You thought you were about to plow an exotic Chinese babe. *Ni hao!*

GALLIMARD: You think I was trying to—?

MARC: Bone a delicate Oriental flower? With your impressive Western manhood?

GALLIMARD: Now you're being disgusting!

MARC: I simply say what you refuse to admit. So you end up here, wanting to stuff your ears with cotton.

GALLIMARD: All right, maybe I . . . in the back of my mind . . . but it was just a passing thought.

MARC: And a great thought that is! Don't let go of it. Just let go of your new friend!

GALLIMARD: What are you telling me to do?

MARC: Leave this excuse for a theatre now. And never return. The good news is, you're in China. Millions of lotus blossoms all around. And you—among a mere handful of men. The kind they all want . . . deep inside.

　　　　(Number ends. Applause)

He's using you. With his preening, flattering. Monsieur Song gains status showing off his Western friend. But you—fraternizing with one of the natives? What would your colleagues think?

　　　　Marc exits. Gallimard follows.

GALLIMARD: Marc? Marc?

SONG: How much of the story did you follow this time?

　　　　They're again backstage, Song changing back
　　　　into the androgynous Mao suit.

GALLIMARD: You were fighting a number of warriors—all of whom I assume were bad guys—um, I had absolutely no idea.

SONG: You are being honest with me. That is a start. Tell me, do you have records?

GALLIMARD: I'm sorry?

SONG: They are forbidden nowadays. You know—Puccini or Edith Piaf or Miles Davis?

GALLIMARD: Oh, phonograph records! Yes, we brought a crate with us to Peking.

SONG: "We"? You mean your wife, yes? Of course you're married. A sophisticated foreign diplomat—with deep blue eyes.

GALLIMARD: Where I come from, almost everyone's eyes are—

SONG: My mother used to play such recordings.

GALLIMARD: Is that how you knew *Madama Butterfly*?

SONG: The opera reminds me of her.

GALLIMARD: I thought you said you hated it.

SONG: Oh, I do. And yet, I love it too. You will learn—I can be very confused.

> (*Song spots an ACTOR, within earshot.*
>
> *Louder*)

A professor of theatre? At the Sorbonne, that's so impressive.

> (*The Actor moves along.*
>
> *Off Gallimard's surprise*)

Come now, we must have a cover story for you, mustn't we? So what were we—? Ah yes, records.

GALLIMARD: I have Piaf. And Gershwin and Serge Gainsbourg and—

SONG: All the most romantic, my favorites! I have a phonograph player. Very up to date, my prized possession. Next week, bring some of your records. You pick. Then we can listen together.

Song exits. Gallimard moves to a desk, where he stamps or rejects papers, handed to him by a CLERK.

GALLIMARD:

(To us)

But I didn't go back. Next week, or the one after. Perhaps Marc was right. My relationship—with Song Liling—there was simply no longer any profit in it.

(Pause)

For the next five weeks, I worked like a dynamo. I felt certain, in time, that my interest in my new friend would fade. And perhaps Song Liling would quickly forget me as well. But after four weeks, they began to arrive. The letters.

Upstage special area on Song, in the Mao suit.

SONG: "Did we fight? I do not know. Is the opera no longer of interest to you? Please come—my audiences miss the white devil in their midst."

GALLIMARD: How ridiculous I had been to sneak around the back alleys of Peking, all for the sake of such a "friendship."

The Clerk hands Gallimard a second letter.

SONG: "Six weeks have passed since we last met. Is this your practice—to leave friends in the lurch?"

GALLIMARD: It's not that we shouldn't make friends with the locals. They can prove useful informants.

A third letter.

SONG: "I suspect there has been some misunderstanding between us. One which could be easily cleared up in a few short moments."

GALLIMARD: But an actor can't tell us much.

SONG: "Come to my flat."

GALLIMARD: Excuse me?

SONG: "I have a secret to share with you."

SCENE 10

Song Liling's apartment.

GALLIMARD: I told myself that I owed him this much—a final word. A cursory farewell. And I'd never before seen the inside of a Chinese flat.

SONG:

(*Offstage*)

SONG (CONT.): I will be out in an instant. Ask the servant for anything you want.

> *(A SERVANT enters, pours Gallimard some tea, then scurries away.*
>
> *Gallimard looks around the room. He picks up a picture in a frame, studies it. Song enters, dressed elegantly in a pre-revolutionary qipao. She stands in the doorway looking like Anna May Wong)*

That is my father.

GALLIMARD: Oh!

> *Gliding up to him, she snatches up the picture.*

SONG: It is very good that he did not live to see the revolution. They would, no doubt, have made him kneel on broken glass.

GALLIMARD: Is this . . . ?

SONG: Not that he didn't deserve such a punishment. Who knows? Perhaps I would've been happy to see it happen.

GALLIMARD: Is this some sort of performance?

SONG: Quite the opposite.

GALLIMARD: But—

SONG: Most of my life is a performance. Except onstage, and here. Within the walls of my flat. Alone. Most of the time. And now, with you.

GALLIMARD: I'm afraid I don't understand.

SONG: But you do. All along, you have known. From the first time you called me "mademoiselle."

GALLIMARD: What are you saying?

SONG: Mine is such an unlikely story. One of the reasons I have never shared it with anyone. I would face ridicule, rejection, and with China being what it is today—even arrest.

GALLIMARD: Arrest? What—?

SONG: Can you understand that a woman's place here—despite this loud, often vulgar, revolution—remains today as it has been for thousands of years?

GALLIMARD: Despite the propaganda that claims—

SONG: That "women hold up half the sky"? On our backs, perhaps. Chairman Mao keeps a harem of underage girls—just like the emperors of old. Nothing has really changed.

   (Pause)

When my mother became pregnant with me, she had already given birth to my three sisters. Father threatened to take another wife unless she produced a son. But sadly, I was born a girl.

GALLIMARD: What?

SONG: My mother begged my father and he agreed: They would dress me as a boy, and that is how I would live. For the rest of my life.

GALLIMARD: Wait. So you're telling me that you are . . . ?

SONG: A woman. What you see onstage is who I really am.

GALLIMARD: But how—?

SONG: This part may be difficult for you to understand.

GALLIMARD: It's *all* difficult to understand!

SONG: Touché. My father wanted a son. Maybe if I'd been born in the West, I would've been cherished.

GALLIMARD: You must appreciate, this is—very hard to believe.

SONG: In your world, certainly. But here in China, it is not so impossible. As the ancient stories tell us.

GALLIMARD: But you live here in Peking now. Away from your parents. Why not just declare the truth?

SONG: It's not that simple. My papers, all my documents, list me as a male. At this point, I would be accused of deceiving the government. Thrown in jail. Besides, in a way, my parents did me a favor. I have known such advantages, living as a man. For instance, my entire career. So I never felt any reason to tell the truth. Until now.

GALLIMARD: Who else have you told about this?

SONG: Nobody. Only you.

GALLIMARD: But why me?

SONG: You're safe. Who could you tell? You can't even speak Chinese. I'm teasing. The truth is, I've wanted to tell you. From the first time we met. Why do you think I wanted you to see *Butterfly Lovers*? Because it is my story. Like that girl, I felt you knew me. That somehow, you could see through my disguises.

GALLIMARD: I thought you despised me.

SONG: Perhaps I did, for a moment. But afterwards, I realized I had pushed you away—because part of me wanted to pull you close. And how terribly dangerous that would be.

(Song starts to refill tea for Gallimard)

What I do, even pouring the tea for you now . . . it has . . . implications.

(She hands Gallimard the tea. Gallimard puts his hand over both the teacup and Song's hand)

Have I made a mistake, revealing myself to a foreign devil?

GALLIMARD: No, Mademoiselle Song. Now it all makes sense.

SONG: I can be myself?

GALLIMARD: Yes.

Gallimard leans in. Song pulls away.

SONG: What are you doing?

GALLIMARD: Hold still. Do you trust me?

(Gallimard leans in. Song does not pull away. Gallimard kisses Song—on the forehead)

I will keep your secret.

SCENE 11

GALLIMARD: And so the world began to change. This sad, lovely creature, with her tragic story—and yet, possible, in a land where women were worth so little. She saw in me a man different from those she had known. A man she could trust.

MARC: So! She's a girl! It seems I was wrong.

GALLIMARD: Amazing, isn't it?

MARC: The servant becomes the master, and all that.

GALLIMARD: Still, I've always valued your friendship. You were the most popular guy in our school.

MARC: Well, there's no guarantee of failure in life like popularity in high school. Somehow, I knew I'd end up in the suburbs working for Peugeot, and you'd end up someplace exciting, picking exotic women off the trees. And they say there's no justice.

GALLIMARD: She's not some fruit to be picked, all right?

MARC: No, I suppose she's still ripening.

GALLIMARD: Marc, I'm not going to abuse her trust.

MARC: That's right, you are going to fulfill it.

GALLIMARD: What?

MARC: Isn't that what every woman wants? A man who makes her feel safe?

GALLIMARD: Well . . .

MARC: Then takes her, every night?

GALLIMARD: I knew you were going to go there.

MARC: They don't reveal their secrets until they have already given their hearts.

GALLIMARD: You think . . . she wants me?

MARC: You know the answer.

GALLIMARD: But I'm a married man.

MARC: And an excellent one too. I cheated after . . . six months. Then again and again, until now—three hundred girls in twelve years. And I keep the books at a car factory.

GALLIMARD: I don't think we should hold you up as an example.

MARC: Of course not. My life—it is disgusting! Phooey! Phooey! But you—you are the model husband.

GALLIMARD: Anyway, it's impossible. I'm a foreigner.

MARC: Ah yes. She cannot love you, it is taboo, but something deep inside her heart—she cannot help herself—she must surrender to you. It is her destiny.

GALLIMARD: How do you imagine all this?

MARC: The same way you do. It's an old story. It's in our blood. They fear us, Rene. Their women fear us. And their men—their men hate us. And you know something? They are all correct.

(They spot a light in a window)

MARC (CONT.): There, Rene!

GALLIMARD: It's her window.

MARC: Late at night—it burns. The light—it burns for you.

GALLIMARD: I won't look. It's not respectful.

MARC: We don't have to be respectful. We're foreign devils.

> (*Enter Song, in a sheer robe, looking even
> more femme. In Gallimard's fantasy, this scene
> mirrors the pinup girl sequence. Except Song keeps
> her back towards him. "Un bel dì vedremo"
> creeps in over the speakers.*
>
> *She brushes her hair, does her nighttime
> toilette, as he watches like a voyeur*)

All your life, you've waited for a beautiful girl who would give
herself to you. All your life you've smiled like a saint when
it's happened to every other man you know. And you see
them in magazines and you see them in movies. And you
wonder, what's wrong with me? Will a fantasy girl ever want
me? As the years pass, your hair thins, and you struggle to
hold on to even your hopes.

> (*Song undoes her gown, lets it fall to the
> ground. They catch a glimpse of her naked
> backside*)

Stop struggling, Rene. The wait is over.

> *Marc exits. Song turns out the lights in her
> bedroom.*

GALLIMARD: No, I will not take advantage of her.

(Gallimard returns to his office)

GALLIMARD (CONT.): Yet, I could not get those thoughts out of my head. They tormented me, night and day, a fever that would not break.

(Pause)

By the end of the week, I felt sick. I had finally gained the trust of this little flower, and now could think of nothing but abusing it. If there is a God, surely he would punish me now. There must be justice in the world.

(Pause)

Sure enough, the ax did fall. I was ordered to report to his office.

SCENE 12

Ambassador Toulon's office.

TOULON, the French ambassador, enters.

TOULON: Gallimard! Good to see you.

GALLIMARD:

(To us)

Manuel Toulon. French ambassador to China. I'd only been in his office once before—the day I arrived in Peking. That was also the only time I'd heard him speak my name.

TOULON: Look, there's not much to say. I've liked you. From the day you walked in. You were no leader, but you were tidy and efficient.

GALLIMARD: Thank you, sir.

TOULON: Wait, there's more. Okay, our needs in China are changing. It's embarrassing that we lost Indochina. Someone just wasn't on the ball there. I don't mean you personally, of course.

GALLIMARD: Thank you, sir.

TOULON: The nature of our work here is changing. Some people are just going to have to go. It's nothing personal.

GALLIMARD: Oh.

TOULON: Want to know a secret? Vice-Consul LeBon is being transferred.

GALLIMARD:

(To us)

My immediate superior!

TOULON: And most of his department.

GALLIMARD:

(To us)

Just as I feared! God has seen my evil heart—

TOULON: But not you.

GALLIMARD:

> (To us)

And he's taking her away just as . . .

> (To Toulon)

Excuse me, sir?

TOULON: Scare you? I think I did. Cheer up, Gallimard. I want you to replace LeBon as vice-consul.

GALLIMARD: You—? Well, thank you, sir.

TOULON: Indeed.

GALLIMARD: I . . . accept with great humility.

TOULON: Humility won't be part of the job. You're going to co-ordinate the revamped intelligence division. The Americans have asked us to be their eyes and ears here. A year ago, you would've been out. But over the past few weeks, I don't know how it happened, you've become this new, aggressive, confident . . . thing. And they also tell me you get along with the Chinese. So your timing is fortunate indeed, Gallimard. Congratulations.

> They shake hands. Toulon exits.

GALLIMARD: Vice-consul? Impossible! As I stumbled out of the building, I saw it written across the sky: There is no God. No—say that there is a God. God, who creates Eve to serve Adam. Who blesses Solomon with his harem but ties Jezebel to a burning bed—that God is a man. And he understands. At age twenty-nine, I was suddenly initiated into the way of the world.

SCENE 13

Song Liling's apartment.

Song enters, in a dressing gown.

SONG: Are you crazy?

GALLIMARD: Mademoiselle Song—

SONG: You come here—without warning?

GALLIMARD: It's the most amazing—

SONG: Bang on my door? Scare my servants? Scandalize the neighbors?

GALLIMARD: I've been promoted. To vice-consul!

Pause.

SONG: Of course you have.

GALLIMARD: What do you mean?

SONG: If I may boast, I saw something special in you.

GALLIMARD: Please. How could you—?

SONG: After all, you are an adventurous imperialist. Much more so than any of your colleagues, correct?

GALLIMARD: Well, true. They don't venture far from the diplomatic district. If only they knew what they were missing.

SONG: I think they do. Yet still, they are afraid to go. See? You are so much more than they could ever hope to be.

(*Pause*)

And I am your Butterfly.

(*He starts to kiss her*)

No . . . no . . . gently . . . please, I've never . . .

GALLIMARD: No?

SONG: I've never . . . So how could I . . . ?

GALLIMARD: Then we will go very, very slowly.

SONG: I'm a modest Chinese girl. You will teach me?

GALLIMARD: I will teach you.

SONG: How to make you happy?

GALLIMARD: You've already made me happy.

SONG: Where to touch you?

GALLIMARD: Yes.

SONG: How to kiss?

(*Gallimard gives Song a long kiss*)

Someone might come in.

GALLIMARD: Can't we lock the—?

SONG: The doors have no locks.

GALLIMARD: But then—maybe I shouldn't.

SONG: Please. I've been waiting for you all my life. Turn out the lights.

> *Gallimard turns out the lights. They move to the bed. We hear* Madame Butterfly, *Act One finale.*

SONG: Monsieur Gallimard?

GALLIMARD: Yes, Butterfly?

SONG: "Vieni, vieni!"

SCENE 14

Song Liling's apartment.

GALLIMARD: That first night we spent together was fumbling, groping, finished almost before it started. But it was also the first time I felt desired by someone who truly needed me. I had the power to rescue this poor girl—and for that, she would love me.

> *(Music on a 1950s phonograph player; Song dressed in a* qipao)

So I came again the following week. And the one after that. If I was caught entering or leaving her home, her life might be in danger. I took a route, through backstreets and alleyways, constantly checking to make sure I wasn't being followed.

Until I arrived at the gate to her courtyard. And within her tiny flat, we began to make a world of our own.

SONG: Outside, all I see are people who look like me, wearing the same drab clothes, repeating the same official lines. With you, I feel I can be myself at last.

GALLIMARD: So do I.

SONG: Really?

GALLIMARD: I feel free.

SONG: In China?

GALLIMARD: Well, with you. So, yes, in China. Even the jazz sounds better here than it did at home.

SONG: You know why? Because here, it is forbidden. You know what this music was made for, don't you?

GALLIMARD: Intimate conversation?

SONG: Dancing. In the dark.

GALLIMARD: Oh. Well, I don't . . .

SONG: Oh. Well, I do.

Rising, she holds out her hands to him.

GALLIMARD: You're going to make me look ridiculous.

SONG: No. This will give me the pleasure of teaching you something too.

(They start to dance)

SONG (CONT.): A simple box step.

GALLIMARD: You can barely hear the—

> *He turns up the music.*

SONG: First, you put one hand here. And the other, here.

> *(They dance)*

Now, you lead me. And if I am very good, if my body follows exactly the way you want me to, then you might pull me very close, and your hand might even slip . . . all the way down here. And I will not move it. Then everyone in the club will see—how much I love you.

> *(A noise in the hall, a shadow appears)*

Enough!

> *(She breaks away from him, turns off the music.*
>
> *Sotto voce)*

Thank you, monsieur.

> *She curtseys. He bows.*

GALLIMARD: You are the most beautiful girl in the world.

SONG: But only to you.

GALLIMARD: Lucky me, then. If other men could see you, as you are now, what would happen to me?

SONG: Silly. Even if a thousand men wanted me—

GALLIMARD: Millions! This is China, after all.

SONG: I would still choose you. You are the smartest, most sophisticated—

GALLIMARD: Oh, please—

SONG: Most powerful—

GALLIMARD: Tell me more.

SONG: Consider your work.

GALLIMARD: You don't know anything about my work.

SONG: Then, tell me.

GALLIMARD: Most of it is incredibly dull.

SONG: You are making decisions that change the shape of the world.

GALLIMARD: Not the world. At best, a small corner.

Toulon enters and sits at a desk upstage.

SCENE 15

French embassy.

Gallimard moves downstage, to Toulon's desk. Song remains upstage, watching.

TOULON: And a more troublesome corner is hard to imagine.

GALLIMARD: So, the Americans plan to begin bombing?

TOULON: This is very secret, Gallimard: Yes.

GALLIMARD: But what about ground troops?

TOULON: That is exactly the question they've put to us. Say that repulsive President Johnson sent a few thousand American marines into Indochina. How will the Chinese react?

GALLIMARD: The Chinese will squawk—

TOULON: Uh-huh.

GALLIMARD: —but in their hearts, they don't even like Ho Chi Minh.

TOULON: What a bunch of jerks. Vietnam was our colony. Not only didn't the Americans help us fight to keep it, but now, seven years later, they've come back to grab the territory for themselves. It's very irritating.

GALLIMARD: With all due respect, sir, why should the Americans have won our war for us back in '54 if we didn't have the will to win it ourselves?

TOULON: You're kidding, aren't you?

GALLIMARD: The Orientals simply want to be associated with whoever shows the most strength and power. You live with the Chinese, sir. Do you think they like Communism?

TOULON: I live in China. Not with the Chinese.

GALLIMARD: Excuse me?

TOULON: *You* live with the Chinese.

GALLIMARD: What are you saying?

TOULON: Only that I'm not immune to gossip. I've received reports. That you leave the foreign sector for an hour or more. Whereabouts unknown.

(*Pause*)

Are you keeping a native mistress?

GALLIMARD: What makes you jump to that conclusion?

TOULON: Hope?

(*Pause*)

What you do on your own time is your business alone.

(*Pause*)

I'm sure she must be gorgeous.

GALLIMARD: Well . . .

TOULON: I'm impressed. You have the stamina to go out into the streets and hunt one down. Some of us have to be content with the wives of the expatriate community.

GALLIMARD: I . . . wasn't aware of that, sir.

TOULON: Perhaps you should offer tutorials. Just be careful—

GALLIMARD: Yes?

TOULON: —that she doesn't expect you to take her back to France!

GALLIMARD: Of course not!

TOULON: So, Gallimard, you've got the inside knowledge—what *do* the Chinese think?

GALLIMARD: Deep down, they miss the old days. My friend even mentioned martinis, men in tuxedos—

TOULON: So what do we tell the Americans about Vietnam?

GALLIMARD: A token display of force will not get the job done.

TOULON: Their general, a fellow named Westmoreland, has requested even more troops: 100,000.

GALLIMARD: He's correct. This war could be over in a year. Orientals will always submit to a greater force.

TOULON: I'll note your opinions in my report. The Americans always love to hear how "welcome" they'll be.

He starts to exit.

GALLIMARD: Sir?

TOULON: Mmmm?

GALLIMARD: Do you think others have reached the same conclusion? About my trips into the city?

TOULON: Gossip is the only pleasure we've got around here.

GALLIMARD: So I should be more careful.

Toulon shrugs.

TOULON: You don't want any of this to reach your wife's ears, of course.

GALLIMARD: But my colleagues . . . ?

TOULON: Let's just say, it never hurts.

GALLIMARD: What do you mean?

TOULON: You went and found yourself a lotus blossom—and topped us all.

    Toulon exits.

GALLIMARD:

    (To us)

Sure enough, I started to notice my coworkers looking at me differently. With envy, yes, but also, admiration. Which only made them clamor for my regard. And life became better than I ever thought it could be.

    (He starts to move downstage, towards Song)

So, over the—

    (COMRADE CHIN enters. Gallimard backs away)

Wait. Who is that?

SONG: The one you heard about. In the courtroom, during our trial.

GALLIMARD: What's going on here? She's not part of my story.

SONG: Yes, she is. Because she's part of mine.

GALLIMARD: I don't want to see this!

SONG: How can your audience understand what really happened— without understanding me?

GALLIMARD:

> *(To us)*

Please—try to see this from my point of view. We are all prisoners of our time and place.

> *He starts to exit.*

SONG: You should stay, Rene. And watch.

> *Gallimard remains onstage.*

SCENE 16

Song Liling's apartment. Beijing. 1966.

CHIN: What we need to know is what Vietnamese cities the Americans plan to bomb.

SONG: I doubt he has such information.

CHIN: Are you capable of this job or not? What else?

SONG: The Americans will increase troops in Vietnam to 170,000 soldiers with 120,000 militia and 11,000 American advisers.

> *Chin takes notes.*

CHIN: How do you remember so much?

SONG: I'm an actor.

CHIN: It is good. That you turn your decadent skills to serve the revolution.

SONG: I am grateful that even an actor can be of some use to our chairman.

CHIN: We know what you have been doing.

SONG: I have no secrets, Comrade.

CHIN: Show them to me.

SONG: I don't . . .

CHIN: Your costumes. I want to see them.

SONG: Is this really necessary?

CHIN: Go!

>   *(Song retrieves a* qipáo *from a closet or trunk)*

Disgusting.

>   *(Pause)*

Bring it here.

>   *Chin feels the fabric.*

CHIN: So flimsy. What is this called?

SONG: Lace. And that is appliqué.

CHIN: It reeks of exploitation.

SONG: I am ashamed to own such bourgeois filth.

CHIN: As well you should be. You should be forced to self-criticize. Thrown into jail. Paraded through the streets.

SONG: But—

CHIN: What?

SONG: Then how could I carry out my duties? For our great helmsman, Chairman Mao?

CHIN: Follow the Communist Party forever! Follow Chairman Mao forever!

SONG:

>   *(Overlapping)*

Follow Chairman Mao forever!

CHIN: Now, get that out of my sight!

SONG: Gladly, Comrade Chin.

CHIN: Dealing with Westerners is a decadent business. I do not envy you, Comrade.

SONG: But it is joyful to serve the state.

CHIN: Yes, of course. Good-bye, Comrade.

>   *(She starts to exit)*

Comrade?

SONG: Yes?

CHIN: Don't forget: There is no homosexuality in China!

SONG: I do not even know what you mean.

CHIN: Good. Continue in your ignorance.

>   *Chin exits.*

Gallimard moves downstage.

GALLIMARD: I don't want to see that woman. Ever again.

SONG: That was always how I felt too.

Song exits.

SCENE 17

GALLIMARD:

(*To us*)

That part of the story—was not necessary. Yes, her life in China
was hard. But it works out for her, you'll see.

(*Pause*)

We couldn't meet often. God knows, it was difficult enough for
me to move through the streets without attracting attention.
We couldn't risk arousing suspicions that she was actually a
woman. But of course, a man entertaining another man too
often in his flat—that would be dangerous as well.

*Song remains onstage, listening, as Agnes
enters.*

AGNES: Rene, I visited Dr. Bolleart this morning.

GALLIMARD: Why? Are you ill?

AGNES: No, no. You see, I wanted to ask him . . . that question
we've been discussing.

GALLIMARD: And I told you, it's only a matter of time. Why did you bring a doctor into this? We just have to keep trying—like a crapshoot, actually.

AGNES: I went, I'm sorry. But listen: He says there's nothing wrong with me.

GALLIMARD: You see? Now, will you stop—?

AGNES: So I made an appointment for you to go in and take some tests.

GALLIMARD: Just like that? Without even asking me?

AGNES: I know it was presumptuous, but—

GALLIMARD: You know, Bolleart is a general practitioner. How much does he really know about these issues?

AGNES: I don't ask for much. One trip! One visit! And then, whatever you want to do about it—you decide.

GALLIMARD: I don't have time for this!

AGNES: Whatever he finds—if he finds nothing, we decide what to do about nothing! But go!

GALLIMARD: I am so busy with Indochina!

AGNES: No, you're just afraid!

(Pause)

I'm sorry.

GALLIMARD: Fine. If it's so important to you. I'll see Bolleart.

Agnes: Only if you want a child, Rene. We have to face the fact that time is running out. Only if you want a child.

She exits.

Gallimard: I'm a modern man, Butterfly. And yet, I don't want to go. I feel like God himself is laughing at me if I can't produce a child.

Song: You men of the West—you're obsessed by your odd desire for equality. Your wife can't give you a child, and you're going to the doctor?

Gallimard: Well, you see, she's already gone.

Song: And because this incompetent can't find the defect, you now have to subject yourself to him? It's unnatural.

Gallimard: You're right, he's not a specialist! Really, what kind of doctor takes a posting in the world's most depressing city?

Song: Would you like to know why your wife can't conceive?

Gallimard: You're going to tell me?

Song: Because you don't love her.

Gallimard:

    (Amused)

I didn't know love was a prerequisite for procreation.

Song: But you don't, do you? Love her?

    (Pause)

SONG (CONT.): Which means . . . you don't have many opportunities, do you?

GALLIMARD: It was a . . . marriage of convenience.

SONG: They all are, aren't they? Marriage is a charade performed by two people upon a stage. Two people who fool themselves into believing their love will never die. That their hearts will never shrivel into a cold, dead thing.

GALLIMARD: Were you ever—married?

SONG: They tried—my parents—to force a woman upon me. I ran away. And devoted my life to the theatre.

GALLIMARD: You gave up on love.

SONG: And now, it surprises me. So much so that even I believe it can last . . . forever.

GALLIMARD: You're not—thinking we could ever be married, are you?

SONG: Haven't you been listening? I am more than content to serve as your mistress. For you see, I do. I do love you. And I also know—that marriage is the death of love.

> *Gallimard and Song kiss deeply. Gallimard*
> *starts to caress her. Then to undress her.*

SONG: No. I can't— You see. It's that time.

GALLIMARD: Of course.

SONG: Wait. Sit. Let me.

SCENE 18

The lights dim. Party noises. An Embassy party and a dormitory for foreign students. Beijing. 1968.

Gallimard expounds before a small group, including RENEE, a female student.

GALLIMARD: So I tell the Americans, stay the course. The Tet offensive was a disaster for the Communists! The worst possible thing would be to show weakness now, when you are so close to bringing freedom. Americans. They do have a tendency to pull out prematurely.

    Toulon enters.

TOULON: Gallimard! Something I forgot to mention at the office.

GALLIMARD:

    (To others)

Excuse me.

    (Moves towards Toulon)

Important, sir?

TOULON: Not really. But when you come in on Monday, your office will be downstairs.

GALLIMARD: What? But why?

TOULON: Nothing. Little personnel shuffle. Durand will be serving for a time as vice-consul.

GALLIMARD: You're replacing me?

TOULON: I wouldn't put it that way. This wasn't my choice, Gallimard. Just following orders. Oh—Ambassador Swanson! I'd better—

GALLIMARD: Wait!

TOULON: Please. You're actually going to make me—?

GALLIMARD: I think I deserve an explanation!

TOULON: For Christ's sake, Gallimard! Very well. The American war is a disaster!

GALLIMARD: It's far too early to—

TOULON: Early? You said a year. There are now hundreds of thousands of troops in Vietnam. Four hundred thousand dollars is being spent for every Viet Cong killed. So Westmoreland's remark that the Oriental does not value life the way Americans do is oddly accurate.

GALLIMARD: But I think the end is in sight.

TOULON: You do not want to quote Johnson, trust me. Paris has lost all faith in his assurances. And yours. They want someone new at your post—someone who actually understands China.

> *Toulon exits. Gallimard stands for a long moment. Then, as a SERVER passes, he takes a whole bottle from the tray.*

RENEE: It's good to see someone taking charge around here.

> (*Renee crosses to him, holding out her empty flute*)

On second thought . . .

> (*She reaches for his bottle. He lets her drink from it directly*)

Chin-chin!

GALLIMARD: And what brings you to the Proletarian Paradise?

RENEE: I'm a student. My father exports a lot of useless stuff to the third world.

GALLIMARD: How useless?

RENEE: You know. Squirt guns, confectioners' sugar, Hula-Hoops . . .

GALLIMARD: I'm sure they appreciate the sugar.

RENEE: I'm here for two years to study Chinese.

GALLIMARD: Two years?

RENEE: That's what everybody says.

GALLIMARD: How do you stand it here? An attractive girl like you?

RENEE: I like it. It's primitive, but . . . well, this is the place to learn Chinese, so here I am.

GALLIMARD: Why Chinese?

RENEE: I think it'll be important someday.

GALLIMARD: Well, maybe we can help move them into the twentieth century. Though they're so damnably arrogant. China's history has been one disaster after another.

RENEE: Not before.

GALLIMARD: When?

RENEE: You know, back when Marco Polo was around.

GALLIMARD: Granted. China was once great.

RENEE: Then the missionaries came, and everything went to hell. That's my theory.

GALLIMARD: True, Madame Chiang in China, Madame Nhu in Vietnam, were both converts, and they both ruled their husbands. Oriental women—when they're good, they're very good, but when they're bad, they're Christian.

RENEE:

(Laughing)

You know what I *don't* like about China?

GALLIMARD: No—what?

RENEE: Nothing to do at night.

GALLIMARD: You come to parties at embassies like everyone else.

RENEE: Yeah, but they get out at ten. And then what?

GALLIMARD: I'm afraid the Chinese idea of a dance hall is a dirt floor and a man with a flute.

RENEE: You're the guy with a Chinese mistress, right?

GALLIMARD: I shouldn't say.

RENEE: Wanna come up to my flat for a drink?

GALLIMARD: All right.

RENEE: I'll meet you outside. Oh—what's your name?

GALLIMARD: Gallimard. Rene.

RENEE: Weird. I'm Renee too.

She exits.

GALLIMARD:

(To us)

It was Butterfly who I longed to see. But we hadn't made arrangements for tonight. And so, I prepared to embark on my first extra-extramarital affair.

He meets Renee in her room.

RENEE: I don't think it's possible to live here without secrets.

GALLIMARD: Honesty can be highly overrated.

RENEE: Do you believe in love?

GALLIMARD: I believe in passion.

He takes Renee's hand. Leans in. They start to make out.

RENEE: You want to know my secret? I think I'm falling in love—

GALLIMARD: Yes?

RENEE: With a Chinese man.

(She starts to undress)

My teacher. At the Foreign Language Institute. I thought he was paying extra attention to me because I was so far behind.

GALLIMARD: I'm sure that was not the reason.

RENEE: But before I knew it—he took me. One night, to the park. It was pitch-black, but I could hear other lovers around us. In the bushes. Apparently, that's where all the students go. Then he laid me down on the grass, undid my blouse, and—god, the things he did to me—with his mouth, his hands, his teeth—teasing me, so slowly, until I—

(Renee's nearly naked when Gallimard leaves)

Wait. Where are you going?

Lights out on Renee.

SCENE 19

Song Liling's flat.

Gallimard enters. She emerges in a negligee and dressing gown.

SONG: Oh! Rene . . . we didn't make—

GALLIMARD: "Make arrangements"? I decided to come over. Is that acceptable to you?

SONG: Of course. If it all were up to me. But—

GALLIMARD: But it's not up to you.

SONG: So we must be—

GALLIMARD: It's up to me.

He grabs Song roughly.

SONG: Have you been drinking?

GALLIMARD: I want to see you naked.

SONG: What?

GALLIMARD: You heard me. Don't pretend.

SONG: I thought you understood—

GALLIMARD: Yes, I have—

SONG: —my modesty.

GALLIMARD: —for long enough! No other man would have put up—

SONG: "Put up"?

GALLIMARD: —with your rules, your restrictions—for all these—

SONG: You've "put up" with me?

GALLIMARD: But as of tonight—no more!

SONG: I thought you understood my shame.

GALLIMARD: Ah, but you gave me your shame! Many years ago.

SONG: What are you—?

GALLIMARD: "I am your Butterfly!" You gave all that to me. Isn't it true?

SONG: Oh, I see.

GALLIMARD: Good.

SONG: I thought myself—

GALLIMARD: Then obey me.

SONG: —so repulsed by the Butterfly story.

GALLIMARD: Strip!

SONG: And now—look—you have become my Lieutenant Pinkerton.

GALLIMARD: Yes, I am.

SONG: The worst part of him!

GALLIMARD: I'm Pinkerton!

SONG: Now I see. We are always most repulsed by what we may one day become.

GALLIMARD: Stop it! Just stop it! I am so sick of the submissive language, the soft lights, the silks, the poetry.

SONG: Really? You no longer wish to be flattered, pleased, seduced?

GALLIMARD: No! Not if—

SONG: What?

GALLIMARD: Not if I'm being lied to! I don't even know what to believe anymore. Is anything real? Here in this fucking inscrutable country? Is anything real here at all?

He breaks the incense burner.

SONG: So what do you want now?

He turns on the light. The room looks ugly.

GALLIMARD: To see. Everything. In the light, with open eyes. I want to see what I'm dealing with here. Who you are.

(Pause)

Take it off. I'm ordering you.

SONG: You know something, Rene?

GALLIMARD: Stop talking!

SONG: I want that too. In fact, it's all I ever wanted. For you to see me. As I am.

(Pause)

But you must do this yourself. Go ahead. Ignore my rules, my restrictions, my modesty. Everything that has made it possible for me to love you. Yes, you will see me. And you will also show us both—who you really are.

Gallimard tears the dressing gown off her.
Looks her in the eye. Reaches for her negligee.
Then his hands slowly drop.

GALLIMARD:

   (To us)

Why did I not undress her? Perhaps because—happiness is so rare that our mind can turn somersaults to protect it.

   (Pause)

At the time, I only knew that I saw Pinkerton stripping the garments from his Butterfly, rewarding her love with his wicked hands. That image sickened me, pulled me to my knees, until I was kneeling before her as if in supplication. And when I looked again at her pure, innocent face, Pinkerton suddenly . . . vanished from my heart. To be replaced by something new, something unnatural, that flew in the face of all I'd learned in the world—something very close to love.

   He grabs her around the waist; she strokes his
hair.

GALLIMARD: Butterfly, forgive me.

SONG: Rene . . .

GALLIMARD: For everything. From the start.

SONG: I'm . . .

GALLIMARD: Yes?

SONG: I'm pregnant.

(Beat)

Song (cont.): I'm pregnant.

(Beat)

I'm pregnant.

BLACKOUT

END OF ACT ONE

ACT TWO

SCENE 1

Song Liling's flat.

We reprise the moment before the act break.

He grabs her around the waist; she strokes his hair.

SONG: I'm pregnant.

GALLIMARD: I want to marry you!

> *Time jump. Song paces as Comrade Chin takes notes. Gallimard watches the scene.*

SONG: I need a baby.

CHIN: What?

SONG: I need a baby.

CHIN: I don't understand.

SONG: I need a baby.

CHIN: What baby? Whose baby?

SONG: Tell Comrade Kang—last night, the entire mission, it could've ended.

CHIN: Last night?

SONG: Tell Kang—he told me to strip.

CHIN: Strip?!

SONG: Write it down! He told me to strip, and I took a chance. Oh, we Chinese, we know how to gamble.

CHIN: Careful, Comrade.

SONG: My palms were wet. I had to make a split-second decision.

CHIN: Before you say something I cannot hear!

SONG: *I'm* the one who's valuable to the chairman! Suddenly, it hit me—this is the moment to find out if he is truly devoted. To the revolution.

CHIN: And?

SONG: If I can present him with a baby. A Chinese baby with blond hair—we will ensure his future cooperation!

CHIN: That is the part I find troubling. The trading of babies has to be a counterrevolutionary act!

SONG: Sometimes, a counterrevolutionary act is necessary to counter a counterrevolutionary act.

CHIN: I don't believe the chairman ever said that.

SONG: I need one in seven months. Make sure it's a boy.

CHIN: You'd better talk to Comrade Kang yourself.

SONG: I will.

>*Chin gets up to leave.*

SONG: Comrade Chin? Why, in the Peking Opera, are women's roles played by men?

CHIN: That is changing. A reactionary remnant of male—

SONG: No.

>*(Beat)*

Because only a man knows how a woman is supposed to act.

>*Chin exits.*

GALLIMARD:

>*(To Song)*

Why are you forcing them to see all this? You're making a mockery of our story!

SONG: I'm telling the truth.

GALLIMARD: The truth! The truth is you betrayed me!

SONG: And you really think I had a choice?

GALLIMARD: You didn't have to lie to me! From the start!

SONG: That's not how we—

GALLIMARD: And yet, I could forget all your deception. If you'd just come back. And become my Butterfly again.

SONG: If you want that, you'll have to see much more than you ever have before.

>   *(Points to us)*

So you were telling your audience about the night I announced I was pregnant.

>   *Gallimard and Song once again resume their*
>   *positions from the end of Act One.*

SCENE 2

GALLIMARD: I'll divorce my wife. We'll live together here, and then later in France.

SONG: I had begun to lose faith. And now, you surprise me with your generosity.

GALLIMARD: Generosity? You're crazy.

SONG: I'm happy. Which often looks like crazy.

GALLIMARD: I can leave my wife. You can live in my flat—to the world, as my friend.

SONG: A foreigner—living with a native man—in China? Better things remain as they are.

GALLIMARD: Then I'll take you to France. Yes, you can finally live as you were meant to be. I'll request a transfer. If necessary, leave the foreign service!

SONG: You would come to hate me.

GALLIMARD: No!

SONG: We Chinese are realists.

GALLIMARD: That's not being realistic. That's defeating yourself before you begin.

SONG: We must conserve our strength for the battles we can win.

GALLIMARD: I don't care!

SONG: You do. So do I. I'm worthy to love and even to be loved by you. But I am not worthy to end the career of one of the West's most promising diplomats.

> *Pause.*

GALLIMARD: They're replacing me. I've been demoted.

SONG: If so, they are even greater fools than I imagined.

GALLIMARD: They say I'm wrong about China. About Vietnam. About everything.

SONG: Who knows more? Some bureaucrats in Paris? Or you? Who know truths they could not even begin to imagine.

> *She exits.*

GALLIMARD:

> *(To us)*

Butterfly went away for several months—to her home village, in Yunnan Province. Her father had died, and her mother agreed to help deliver . . . our baby. I waited anxiously in Peking. Until the night she called for me.

> *A baby's cry from offstage. Song enters,*
> *carrying a child.*

SONG: He looks like you.

GALLIMARD: Oh!

> *(Beat; he approaches the baby)*

Well, babies are never very attractive at birth.

SONG: Stop!

GALLIMARD: I'm sure he'll grow more beautiful with age. More like his mother.

SONG: Would you like to hold him?

GALLIMARD: I have a son.

> *(Gallimard holds the baby)*

Oh my god. This feeling—

SONG: He is fortunate—to have a foreign father.

GALLIMARD: And a famous mother.

SONG: No. Soon, I'm afraid, my fame will count against me.

GALLIMARD: Why?

SONG: China is changing. They are taking away every last remnant of an older way of life. They even are taking away the opera.

GALLIMARD: What do you mean?

SONG: When I returned from Yunnan, I went to the theatre. Everyone I know is gone. Instead, they are performing new dances and stories. Without subtlety or grace. It's terrifying.

    (Pause)

So you see, we must depend on you.

GALLIMARD: Whatever's happening here, don't be afraid. I promise, I will take care of you both.

SCENE 3

Beijing. 1968.

The driving rhythm of Chinese percussion fills the stage.
RED GUARD DANCERS rush onto the stage, performing
one of the new Revolutionary Operas.

GALLIMARD: Overnight, it seemed, the new operas were everywhere. They were the only entertainment now allowed. For Mao had grown very old, and like many old men, entered his second childhood. So he handed over the reins of state to those with minds like his own. And children ruled the Middle Kingdom with complete caprice. The doctrine of the

Cultural Revolution implied continuous anarchy. Butterfly's servant was arrested and we feared would be forced to inform against her.

Toulon enters.

TOULON: Congratulations, Gallimard.

GALLIMARD: Excuse me, sir?

TOULON: You're getting what we all want. You're going home.

GALLIMARD: What?

TOULON: You've had four years to prove yourself, that's certainly sufficient.

GALLIMARD: I'm being transferred . . . because I was wrong about the American war?

TOULON: We don't care about the Americans. Everything you've predicted here in the Orient . . . just hasn't happened.

GALLIMARD: I think that's premature.

TOULON: Okay, you said China was ready to open to Western trade. The only thing they're trading out there are Western heads. You said the people here would soon reject Communism. Instead, they're killing each other to prove their ideological purity.

GALLIMARD: This is just a phase; it will pass.

TOULON: Don't be pathetic. And don't take this personally. You were wrong. It's not your fault.

GALLIMARD: But I'm going home.

TOULON: Right. Could I have the number of your mistress?

> (*Beat*)

Joke! Joke! Think—you'll actually get to eat a salad again.

> *Toulon exits.*

GALLIMARD: I'm leaving China! I can finally take her with me. She can live her true life—at last! I rushed to her flat, to deliver the good news . . . only to find nothing, all her possessions gone.

SCENE 4

> *Dancers drag Song, wearing a Mao suit, onto the stage. They carry a banner reading: "The Actor Renounces His Decadent Profession!" They make Song kneel.*

> *Comrade Chin enters.*

CHIN: Actor-oppressor, for years you have lived above the common people and looked down on their labor. While the farmer ate millet—

SONG: I ate pastries from France and sweetmeats from silver trays.

CHIN: And how did you come to live in such an exalted position?

SONG: I was a plaything for the imperialists!

CHIN: What did you do?

SONG: I shamed China by allowing myself to be corrupted by a foreigner.

CHIN: The people demand a full confession!

SONG: Dresses! I owned dresses!

CHIN: What kind?

SONG: Prerevolutionary dresses! Made of flimsy fabric—

CHIN: With lace and appliqué! I felt them with my own fingers. Owning such decadent relics of the Four Olds was bad enough. What did you do with these dresses?

SONG: I wore them.

CHIN: Louder!

SONG: I wore them!

CHIN: I saw this traitor—wearing dresses!

> (Dancers look over, disgusted. As the
> movement resumes, they "beat" Song and
> lampoon the Chinese opera)

So—what do you want to do now?

SONG: I want to serve the people.

> Percussion starts up.

CHIN: What?

SONG: I want to serve the people!

Dancers regain their revolutionary smiles and begin a dance of victory.

CHIN: What?!

SONG: I want to serve the people!

Dancers unveil a banner: "The Actor Is Rehabilitated!" Song remains kneeling before Chin, as the dancers surround them, then exit. Music out.

SCENE 5

Paris. 1968.

Gallimard enters.

GALLIMARD: I knew so little. About any of this, you must understand. I was already back in Paris. Trying to fit back into a world which now felt so foreign. And what was waiting for me there? Well, better Chinese food than I'd eaten in China. Friends and relatives. A little accounting, regular schedule, keeping track of traffic violations in the suburbs ... and the indignity of students shouting the slogans of Chairman Mao at me—in French.

AGNES:

(Offstage)

Rene? Rene?

(She enters, soaking wet)

AGNES (CONT.): I've had a ... a problem.

She sneezes.

GALLIMARD: You're wet.

AGNES: Yes, I ... coming back from the grocer's. A group of students, waving red flags, they—

(Gallimard fetches a towel)

—they ran by. I was caught up along with them. Before I knew what was happening—

(Gallimard gives her the towel)

Thank you. The police started firing water cannons at us. I tried to shout, to tell them I was the wife of a diplomat, but—I doubt they could even hear me ...

(Pause)

Needless to say, I lost the groceries. Rene, what's happening to France?

GALLIMARD: What's—? Well, nothing, really.

AGNES: Nothing?! The storefronts are in flames, there's glass in the streets, buildings are toppling—and I'm wet!

GALLIMARD: Nothing! ... that I care to think about.

AGNES: And is that why you stay in this room?

GALLIMARD: Yes, in fact.

AGNES: With the incense burning? You know something? I hate incense. It smells so sickly sweet.

GALLIMARD: Well, I hate the French. Who just smell—period!

AGNES: Maybe the Chinese were right.

GALLIMARD: Please—don't start.

AGNES: All that propaganda they were screaming—

GALLIMARD: No, no . . .

AGNES: The West is a "paper tiger"—

GALLIMARD: Agnes—

AGNES: The inevitability of world revolution. Well? Doesn't it look like that to you?

GALLIMARD: Agnes! Please!

> *(Pause)*

You have never understood, have you? You walk in here with these ridiculous ideas, that the Chinese hated us. Deep inside, all they want is to be like us. You come in, dripping off the streets, and leave water all over my floor.

> *He grabs Agnes's towel, begins mopping up the floor.*

AGNES: I found the letters. The ones you've been writing. For god knows how long. A huge stack of them. To some Chinese slut. "I swear, I will find a way" . . . "to rescue you from your" . . . You're a clerk! How are you going to rescue anyone, when you haven't even got the courage to drop them in a mailbox?

GALLIMARD: Agnes, I want a divorce!

Pause.

AGNES: Now you wish to be a failure in marriage as well?

GALLIMARD: I've had a mistress.

AGNES: I knew you would. I knew you would the day I married you. And now what? You want to marry her?

GALLIMARD: I can't. She's over there.

AGNES: You want to leave. For someone who's not here, is that right?

GALLIMARD: That's right.

AGNES: You can't live with her, but still you don't want to live with me.

GALLIMARD: That's right.

AGNES: I thought at least I married the kind of man who knew how to keep up appearances.

(Pause)

I never thought I'd say it. But, in China, I was happy. I knew, in my own way, I knew that you were not everything you pretended to be. But the pretense—going on your arm to the embassy ball, visiting your office and the guards saying, "Good morning, good morning, Madame Gallimard"—the pretense . . . was very good indeed.

(Pause)

AGNES (CONT.): I hope one day, the whole world sees you for the fool that you are.

> *She exits.*

GALLIMARD:

> *(To us)*

Prophetic.

SCENE 6

A bar in Paris and a commune in Xinjiang, China.

Marc enters.

GALLIMARD: In China, there was danger, romance. I was different from all other men.

MARC: Sure. You were white. Here's your drink.

GALLIMARD: I felt . . . touched.

MARC: In the head. Rene, I don't want to hear about the Oriental love goddess. Okay? One night—can we just drink and throw up without a lot of conversation?

GALLIMARD: But she's suffering! Because of me!

MARC: Well, you're suffering 'cuz of her. So you're even.

> *Split scene. Song and Chin at a commune on one side, Gallimard and Marc on the other.*

SONG: I've already worked eight years in the fields of Xinjiang, Comrade Chin.

CHIN: So? Farmers work all their lives. Let me see your hands.

(Song holds them out for her inspection)

Goddamn! Still so smooth! You've just spent too many years in luxury to be any good to the revolution.

SONG: I served the revolution. Ask Comrade Kang!

CHIN: The counterrevolutionary traitor Kang has killed himself. In prison. I reported him—for illegal trading in babies.

GALLIMARD: We have a child together!

MARC: So? I have four. At least you don't pay alimony.

CHIN: You treated me like some stupid peasant girl.

GALLIMARD: Have you seen the news? About what's going on over there?

CHIN: But I always knew what was going on.

GALLIMARD: Families have been torn apart, it's utter chaos.

CHIN: The only time you were ever useful was with your Frenchman.

GALLIMARD: She should be here with me.

SONG: What?

GALLIMARD: I was supposed to rescue her.

CHIN: Write him a letter. Convince him.

GALLIMARD: To bring her to Paris!

CHIN: To bring you to Paris! There, you will give us weekly reports! Useful information!

SONG: That's crazy.

MARC: Sure, she'll fit right in over here.

SONG: It's been eight years. He must have forgotten me by now.

GALLIMARD: She must hate me.

CHIN: You better hope he hasn't. Go. Write.

MARC: It's called the white man's burden, Rene.

CHIN: Why in the new China do peasants rule over the elite?

SONG: I don't know.

CHIN: Because only peasants know where China's rot truly lies.

    Chin exits. Song writes.

MARC: Think a whore would help?

GALLIMARD: Are you listening to a word I'm saying?

MARC: I try not to. But you're so fucking persistent. Look, you're driving me away. I'm leaving.

    (Pause)

Some kids who are losers—just stay that way for life.

    Marc exits.

GALLIMARD:

>*(To us)*

This is the ultimate cruelty, isn't it? That I can talk and talk and to anyone listening, it's only air—too rich a diet to be swallowed by a mundane world. Why can't anyone understand? That in China, I once loved, and was loved by, very simply, the Perfect Woman.

>*Gallimard receives a letter. He reads it.*

SONG:

>*(Offstage)*

"Many years have passed, and I have spent each moment yearning for my foreign husband, that he will come back to me. Do you still remember your Butterfly? I pray you do, for you are the only man who can save me from my people. Please. Bring me to Paris."

GALLIMARD: At last! All these years, I have remained true. In the face of doubt, ridicule, even persecution. My old friends here have mocked and abandoned me, all because I refused to forget her.

>*(Pause)*

Now I will fulfill my promise. Save her at last. And prove that my heart is pure—that love can survive, across oceans, and continents, and time.

>*"Un bel dì vedremo" begins to play over the speakers. Song enters, from a distance, in a long cross, dressed as a beautiful woman.*

SONG: Rene?

GALLIMARD: My imagination is hell. Are you really—?

SONG: Rene. I'm here. Touch me.

GALLIMARD: Why? So you can disappear again and leave me clutching at the air? For the entertainment of my neighbors, who—?

> *Song touches Gallimard.*

SONG: Rene?

GALLIMARD: Butterfly? I never doubted you'd return.

SONG: I was afraid . . . that you had forgotten.

GALLIMARD: Yes, actually, I've forgotten everything. My mind, you see—there wasn't enough room in this hard head—not for the world and for you. No, there was only room for one.

SONG: I . . . I don't know what to say.

GALLIMARD: There's nothing to say. Not at the end of a long trip. Can I make you some tea?

SONG: But where's your wife?

GALLIMARD: She's by my side. She's by my side at last.

> *Gallimard reaches to embrace Song. Song moves away. Music out.*

SONG:

> *(To us)*

So I did return to Rene in Paris. Where I found—

GALLIMARD: Why do you run away? Can't we show them how we embraced that evening?

SONG: We can leave that to their imaginations.

GALLIMARD: This is where I show them! How I rescued you in the end! Brought you to France! Where you were finally free!

SONG: Free? Is that what you believe?

GALLIMARD: Free to live openly—as who you were always meant to be.

SONG: No. Free to live—as who *you* wanted me to be. Introduced to friends and strangers alike as Mademoiselle Song.

GALLIMARD: Yes, that's what I mean. Plus, you became a celebrity!

SONG: In your mind, perhaps.

GALLIMARD: You were able to perform your opera once again. The aria from *Butterfly Lovers*. A dance from *Madame White Snake*.

SONG: Before audiences who had no idea what they were seeing. For all they knew, I could've been performing the death scene from *Madama Butterfly*.

GALLIMARD: So you'd rather I have let you rot? In that labor camp? Would this have made you happier?

SONG: I'd rather you had seen me. Even once.

GALLIMARD: I don't know what you're talking about.

SONG: For who I really am.

GALLIMARD: I'm the only person in the world who ever really loved you.

SONG: Then prove it. Don't let the story end here. With our "grand reunion." For once, show them—what happened afterwards.

GALLIMARD: No.

SONG: Just a few years later.

GALLIMARD: I don't— It's not important.

SONG: It's the most important part—of *our* story.

GALLIMARD: All right. This is over. It's over.

> *Waves his hands. Lights switch. Stage goes bare.*

SONG: Rene.

GALLIMARD:

> *(To us)*

I'm sorry. My apologies. Something's gone terribly wrong. For some reason I don't understand, matters have spiraled out of my control.

SONG: Exactly.

GALLIMARD: I'm leaving. I will begin again—another evening.

> *He starts to exit. Then—*

Two French DST counterintelligence
AGENTS enter. Song exits.

AGENT 1: Rene Gallimard?

GALLIMARD: Wait. Who are you?

AGENT 1: We're from the DST.

GALLIMARD: I don't— What's going on here?

AGENT 2: Please come with us.

GALLIMARD: But I already decided. This story is over.

AGENT 1: I'm afraid it's not, sir. We're placing you under arrest. On the charge of espionage.

GALLIMARD: This can't be happening.

AGENT 1: We're already questioning your accomplice, Monsieur Song.

GALLIMARD: Wait. Who?

AGENT 1: Monsieur Song Liling. He is currently making a full confession.

GALLIMARD: Who? She was standing right—

AGENT 1: Your housemate. Monsieur Song. Now, come with us. Or we'll be forced to—

GALLIMARD: You've got the wrong idea. My housemate, Song Liling, is a woman.

AGENT 1: That can't possibly be your defense, Monsieur Gallimard.

GALLIMARD: She may say she's a man. But that's not the truth.

Agent 2 reveals himself to be Marc.

MARC: No, no, no, Rene!

GALLIMARD: Marc?

MARC: You're really going to say that? In public?

GALLIMARD: I can explain everything!

MARC: Oh god. If anyone asks, I'll have to tell people I never knew you.

GALLIMARD: What are you talking about?

MARC: Now the world is about to find out. And so will you.

The Agents take Gallimard away.

SCENE 7

A courtroom in Paris. 1986.

Song is dressed as a man, in a well-cut suit.

SONG: So I'd played my part better than I had a right to expect. Rene remembered; he applied for me to emigrate to France. Far beyond anything I had hoped, or even believed possible. All the things Westerners in Asia are told never to do for their "native lovers." And then there was the spying.

*(Song moves upstage, to a chair. Toulon
becomes a JUDGE. Song testifies in a courtroom.
Gallimard is brought in to watch)*

SONG (CONT.): I told Rene that the Chinese government had our son. That they would only protect him if we agreed to pass along secrets. But Rene had lost all his high-level contacts. Comrade Chin wasn't very interested in parking-ticket statistics. So he got a job as a diplomatic courier, handling sensitive documents. He'd photograph them for me, and I'd pass them on to the Chinese embassy.

JUDGE: Did he understand the extent of his activity?

SONG: He did it for our child.

JUDGE: He must've known he was passing classified information.

SONG: At this point in his career, he didn't have much love left for the diplomatic corps.

JUDGE: And did he also know you had been passing secrets to the Chinese? From the very beginning of your time together in Peking?

SONG: No. He didn't know about that. That wasn't his fault.

    Pause.

JUDGE: There is one more thing that the court—indeed, all of France—would like to know.

SONG: I wonder what that might be?

JUDGE: Did Monsieur Gallimard know you were a man?

SONG: Well, he never saw me completely naked. Ever.

JUDGE: But surely, he must've . . . How can I put this?

SONG: Most of the time, I did all the work. And during those few occasions when he wanted more, I had my methods. But honestly, sex wasn't at the heart of our relationship.

JUDGE: So what was?

SONG: Your Honor, it was necessary to make him think I was a woman. So that is what I did.

JUDGE: Impossible.

SONG: Not really.

JUDGE: What are you? Some sort of magician?

SONG: My mother was a prostitute near the Vietnam border before the revolution. Where she learned a few things about Western men. About how they think. So I borrowed her knowledge.

JUDGE: Would you care to enlighten the court with this secret knowledge? I'm sure we're all very curious.

SONG: I'm sure you are. But does it really matter?

JUDGE: Of course it does! Will you cooperate or not?

SONG: Men always believe what they want to hear. So a girl can tell her lover the most obnoxious lies and he'll believe her every time—"This is my first time"—"That's the biggest I've ever seen"—or both, which, if you really think about it, is not possible in a single encounter. You've maybe heard those phrases a few times in your own life, yes, Your Honor?

JUDGE: It's not my life, Monsieur Song, that is on trial today.

SONG: But you're the one who's curious.

JUDGE: Go on!

SONG: As soon as a Western man comes into contact with the East—he's already confused. The West has sort of an international rape mentality towards the East. Do you know rape mentality?

JUDGE: Give us your definition, please.

SONG: Basically, "Her mouth says no, but her eyes say yes." The West thinks of itself as masculine—big guns, big industry, big . . . well, you know your own fantasies. And so the East is feminine—whether as Butterfly or as wily Dragon Lady—it's inscrutable, exotic, filled with feminine mystique.

(Pause)

Her mouth says no, but her eyes say yes. The West believes the East, deep down, wants to be dominated—because a woman can't think for herself.

JUDGE: You're taking this in a direction entirely different from what I—

SONG: You expect Asian countries to submit to your guns, and you expect Asian women to be submissive to your men. That's why you say they make the best wives.

JUDGE: Please—get to the point. How could Monsieur Gallimard not know?

SONG: One, because when he finally met his fantasy woman, he wanted more than anything to believe that she was, in fact, a woman. And second, I am an Oriental. And being an Oriental, I can never be completely a man.

   Pause.

JUDGE: That's your answer? This armchair political philosophy?

SONG: Yes. That's my answer.

JUDGE: The *république* demands the full truth! We are not here for your amusement!

SONG: Though apparently, I am here for yours.

JUDGE: Did Monsieur Gallimard ever touch your genitals?

SONG: You really want me to—?

JUDGE: Did the two of you have anal intercourse? Or what?

SONG: No, he didn't put it up my ass!

JUDGE: Ugh, disgusting business. But at least we're finally getting somewhere.

SONG: When we fucked, I pushed my balls up into a cavity between my legs, which left my scrotal sack dangling, like the lips of a vulva. I tucked my cock between my balls, held my legs together, and used cooking oil for lubrication. Apparently, when I put all that together, it must have felt like a very shallow pussy. Which is probably what he imagined of a delicate Chinese girl. Anyway, I never got any complaints. And every month, the butcher down the road supplied me with bloody rags, which I left in my trash for him to discover. Is that graphic enough for you?

JUDGE: I still don't . . . completely understand.

SONG: I can't account for your lack of vision.

JUDGE: Just answer my question: Did Monsieur Gallimard know you were a man?

SONG: You know, Your Honor, I never asked. And why should any of this matter to you, if it didn't matter to us? Funny—I thought of the West as the place I'd find freedom.

SCENE 8

Song's wig and kimono have been brought onstage. Gallimard crawls towards them. Song remains in the witness box, delivering a testimony we do not hear.

GALLIMARD:

> *(To us)*

So here I am. Once again, in my moment of greatest humiliation. Exposed, in this courtroom. With that . . . person up there, telling you and the world . . . What strikes me especially is how crude he is, disrespectful, bereft of gratitude . . . So little like my Butterfly.

> *Song suddenly stands straight up in his witness box and looks at Gallimard.*

SONG: Yes. You. White man.

> *Song steps out of the witness box and moves downstage towards Gallimard. Light change.*

GALLIMARD:

> *(To Song)*

Who? Me?

SONG: Do you see any other white men?

GALLIMARD: Yes. There're white men all around. This is a French courtroom.

SONG: I suppose it is. You know, Rene, I'm so tired of France. Why not return? To China? Back where we began.

GALLIMARD:

> *(To us)*

And once again, against my will, I am transported.

> *Chinese opera music comes up on the speakers.*
> *Song begins to do opera moves.*

SONG: Do you remember? Those nights you gave me your heart?

GALLIMARD: That was a long time ago.

SONG: Yet, they remain with us to this day. Nights that turned our worlds upside down.

GALLIMARD: Perhaps.

SONG: Oh, be honest with me. What's another bit of flattery when you've already flattered me for so many years? It's a wonder my head hasn't swollen to the size of China.

GALLIMARD: Who's to say it hasn't?

SONG: Who's to say? And what's so wrong? With pride? You think I would've taken this chance if I wasn't already full of pride when we met? To believe you can will, with your eyes, with your lips, the destiny of another.

(He dances)

You said in France, our fantasies could finally come true. You said in France, we could live as we were meant to be. So let's try something new. Come. You still want me. Even in slacks and a button-down collar.

GALLIMARD: I don't see what the point of—

SONG: You don't? You see, Rene, it makes no difference. Clothes—do not make the man.

He starts to remove his clothes.

GALLIMARD: What—what are you doing?

SONG: Helping you to see through my act.

GALLIMARD: Stop that! I don't want to! I don't—

SONG: Oh, but you asked me to strip, remember?

GALLIMARD: That was years ago! And I took it back!

SONG: We came so close then. But you postponed it. Postponed the inevitable. Today, the inevitable has come calling.

From the speakers, cacophony: Butterfly *mixed in with Chinese gongs.*

GALLIMARD: No! Stop! I don't want to see!

SONG: Then look away.

GALLIMARD: You're only in my mind! All this is in my mind! I order you! To stop!

SONG: To what? To strip? That's just what I'm—

GALLIMARD: No! Stop! I want you—!

SONG: You want me?

GALLIMARD: To stop!

SONG: You know something, Rene? Your mouth says no, but your eyes say yes. Turn them away. I dare you.

GALLIMARD: Every night, I search for a new ending. One more beautiful, not like this!

SONG: This is the ending *I've* been searching for.

GALLIMARD: Why?

SONG: I believe it can lead—to a new beginning.

GALLIMARD: No, it won't. You're going to ruin everything!

SONG: For years, I've been frustrated. For years, I've wanted to scream, "Look at me, you fool!" And now, at last, you will.

He is down to his briefs.

GALLIMARD: Please. This is unnecessary. I know what you are.

SONG: Do you?

GALLIMARD: I knew all the time somewhere that my happiness was temporary, my love a deception. But my mind kept the knowledge at bay. To make the wait bearable.

SONG: Monsieur Gallimard—the wait is over.

> *Song drops his briefs. He is naked. Sound cue*
> *out. Slowly, we and Song come to the realization*
> *that what we had thought to be Gallimard's*
> *sobbing is actually his laughter.*

GALLIMARD: Oh god!

> *He bursts into laughter again.*

SONG: Rene? I fail to see what's so funny!

GALLIMARD: You "fail to see"—! I mean, you never did have much of a sense of humor, did you? I just think it's terribly funny that I've wasted so much time on just a man!

SONG: "Just a man"?

GALLIMARD: Isn't that what you've been trying to convince me of?

SONG: Yes, but what I mean—

GALLIMARD: And now I finally believe you, and you tell me it's not true? I think you must have some kind of identity problem.

SONG: Will you listen to me?

GALLIMARD: Why?! I've been listening to you for years. Don't I deserve a vacation?

SONG: Why should it matter what I am?

GALLIMARD: Well, you must be *something*. Unless you're nothing.

SONG: How can you say—?

*Song picks up Butterfly's robes, starts to dance
around. No music.*

GALLIMARD: Yes, that's very nice. I have to admit.

Song holds out his arm to Gallimard.

SONG: It's the same skin you've worshiped for years. Touch it.

GALLIMARD: Yes, it does feel the same.

SONG: Now—close your eyes.

*Song covers Gallimard's eyes with one hand.
With the other, Song draws Gallimard's hand up
to his face.*

GALLIMARD: This skin, I remember. The curve of her face, the
softness of her cheek, her hair against the back of my
hand . . .

SONG: I'm your Butterfly. Under the robes, beneath everything,
it was always me. Now open your eyes and admit it—you
adore me.

He removes his hand from Gallimard's eyes.

GALLIMARD: You, who knew every inch of my desires—how
could you, of all people, have made such a mistake?

SONG: What?

GALLIMARD: You showed me your true self. When all I loved
was the lie. A perfect lie, which you let fall to the ground—
and now it's old and soiled.

SONG: So—you never really loved me. Only when I was playing a part.

GALLIMARD: I'm a man who loved a woman created by a man. Everything else—simply falls short.

Pause.

SONG: What am I supposed to do now? You've left me in no-man's-land.

GALLIMARD: I have a date . . . with my Butterfly.

SONG: So come back to my—

GALLIMARD: Get away from me! Tonight, I've finally learned to tell fantasy from reality. And, knowing the difference, I choose fantasy.

SONG: I'm your fantasy!

GALLIMARD: You? You're as real as hamburger. Now, get out! I don't want your body polluting the room!

Gallimard tosses Song's suit at him. Song dresses.

SONG: Let's just say . . . I'm disappointed in you, René. In the crush of your adoration, I thought you'd become something more. More like . . . a woman.

(Pause)

But no. Men. You're like the rest of them. Who would rather destroy the world than see beyond the limits of your own mind. You really have so little imagination!

GALLIMARD: You, Monsieur Song? Accuse me of too little imagination? You, if anyone, should know—I am pure imagination. Now, get out!

> *Gallimard bodily removes Song from the stage, taking his kimono.*

SONG: Rene! I'll never put on those robes again! You'll be sorry!

GALLIMARD:

> *(To Song)*

I'm already sorry!

> *(Looking at the kimono in his hands)*

Exactly as sorry . . . as a Butterfly.

SCENE 9

Gallimard's prison cell. Paris. 1986.

GALLIMARD: I've played out the events of my life night after night, always searching for a new ending to my story, one where I leave this cell and return forever to my Butterfly's arms. Tonight I realize my search is over. That I've looked all along in the wrong place. And now, to you, I will prove that my love was not in vain.

> *(Perhaps with the assistance of the Dancers, he starts to transform himself into an image of his Butterfly)*

GALLIMARD (CONT.): There is a vision of the Orient that I have. Of slender women in *qipao*s and kimonos who die for the love of unworthy foreign devils. Who are born and raised to be the perfect women. Who take whatever punishment we give them, and bounce back, strengthened by love, unconditionally. It is a vision that has become my life.

    (He makes up his face)

In public, I have continued to deny that Song Liling is a man. This brings me headlines and is a source of great embarrassment to my French colleagues, who can now be sent into a coughing fit by the mere mention of Chinese food. But alone, in my cell, I have now faced the truth.

    (Pause)

And the truth demands a sacrifice. For mistakes made over the course of a lifetime. My mistakes were simple and absolute— the man I gave my heart to was not what I believed him to be. Our life together was born in lies. And upon this rotting foundation, I built a shining edifice—piece by piece—from all my love.

    (Pause)

Yes—love. Why not admit it? That was my undoing, wasn't it? Love warped my judgment, blinded my eyes, rearranged the very lines on my face . . . until I could look in the mirror and see nothing but . . . a woman.

    (He puts on a Butterfly wig)

I have a vision. Of the Orient. That deep within its almond eyes, there are still women willing to sacrifice themselves for the love of a man. Even a man whose love is completely without worth.

(He dons the kimono. Is handed a knife)

GALLIMARD (CONT.): Death with honor is better than life . . . life with dishonor.

(He sets himself center stage, in a seppuku position)

The love of a Butterfly can withstand many things—unfaithfulness, loss, even abandonment. But how can it face the one tragedy that implies all others? The devastating knowledge that, underneath it all, the object of her love was nothing more, nothing less than . . . a man.

(Pause)

It is 1986. And I have found her at last. In a prison on the outskirts of Paris. My name is Rene Gallimard—also known as Madame Butterfly.

Gallimard commits seppuku, as music from the "Love Duet" blares over the speakers. He collapses onto the floor. The image holds for several beats.

Song enters, as a man, to find the dead Gallimard.

SONG: Butterfly? Butterfly?

Song collapses over the body of Gallimard. Lights FADE TO BLACK.

END OF PLAY

AFTERWORD

It all started in May of 1986, over casual dinner conversation. A friend asked, had I heard about the French diplomat who'd fallen in love with a Chinese actress, who subsequently turned out to be not only a spy, but a man? I later found a two-paragraph story in *The New York Times*. The diplomat, Bernard Bouriscot, attempting to account for the fact that he had never seen his "girlfriend" naked, was quoted as saying, "I thought she was very modest. I thought it was a Chinese custom."

Now, I am aware that this is *not* a Chinese custom, that Asian women are no more shy with their lovers than are women of the West. I am also aware, however, that Bouriscot's assumption was consistent with a certain stereotyped view of Asians as bowing, blushing flowers. I therefore concluded that the diplomat must have fallen in love, not with a person, but with a fantasy stereotype. I also inferred that, to the extent the Chinese spy encouraged these misperceptions, he must have played up to and exploited this image of the Oriental woman as demure and submissive. (In general, by the way, we prefer the term "Asian" to "Oriental," in the same way "Black" is superior to "Negro." I use the term "Oriental" specifically to denote an exotic or imperialistic view of the East.)

I suspected there was a play here. I purposely refrained from further research, for I was not interested in writing docudrama. Frankly, I didn't want the "truth" to interfere with my own speculations. I told Stuart Ostrow, a producer with whom I'd worked before, that I envisioned the story as a musical. I remember going so far as to speculate that it could be some "great *Madame Butterfly*–like tragedy." Stuart was very intrigued, and encouraged me with some early funding.

Before I can begin writing, I must "break the back of the story," and find some angle which compels me to set pen to paper. I was driving down Santa Monica Boulevard one afternoon, and asked myself, "What did Bouriscot think he was getting in this Chinese actress?" The answer came to me clearly: "He probably thought he had found Madame Butterfly."

The idea of doing a deconstructivist *Madame Butterfly* immediately appealed to me. This, despite the fact that I didn't even know the plot of the opera! I knew Butterfly only as a cultural stereotype; speaking of an Asian woman, we would sometimes say, "She's pulling a Butterfly," which meant playing the submissive Oriental number. Yet, I felt convinced that the libretto would include yet another lotus blossom pining away for a cruel Caucasian man, and dying for her love. Such a story has become too much of a cliché not to be included in the archtypal East-West romance that started it all. Sure enough, when I purchased the record, I discovered it contained a wealth of sexist and racist clichés, reaffirming my faith in Western culture.

Very soon after, I came up with the basic "arc" of my play: the Frenchman fantasizes that he is Pinkerton and his lover is Butterfly. By the end of the piece, he realizes that it is he who has been Butterfly, in that the Frenchman has been duped by love; the Chinese spy, who exploited that love, is therefore the real Pinkerton. I wrote a proposal to Stuart Ostrow, who found it very exciting. (On the night of the Tony Awards, Stuart produced my original two-page treatment, and we were gratified to see that it was, indeed, the play I eventually wrote.)

I wrote a play, rather than a musical, because, having "broken the back" of the story, I wanted to start immediately and not be hampered by the lengthy process of collaboration. I would like to think, however, that the play has retained many of its musical roots. So *Monsieur Butterfly* was completed in six weeks between September and mid-October, 1986. My wife, Ophelia, thought *Monsieur Butterfly* too obvious a title, and suggested I abbreviate it in the French fashion. Hence, *M. Butterfly*, far more mysterious and ambiguous, was the result.

I sent the play to Stuart Ostrow as a courtesy, assuming he would not be interested in producing what had become a straight play. Instead, he flew out to Los Angeles immediately for script conferences. Coming from a background in the not-for-profit theatre, I suggested that we develop the work at a regional institution. Stuart, nothing if not bold, argued for bringing it directly to Broadway.

It was also Stuart who suggested John Dexter to direct. I had known Dexter's work only by its formidable reputation. Stuart sent the script to John, who called back the next day, saying it was the best play he'd read in twenty years. Naturally, this predisposed me to like him a great deal. We met in December in New York. Not long after, we persuaded Eiko Ishioka to design our sets and costumes. I had admired her work from afar ever since, as a college student I had seen her poster for *Apocalypse Now* in Japan. By January 1987, Stuart had optioned *M. Butterfly*, Dexter was signed to direct, and the normally sloth-like pace of commercial theatre had been given a considerable prod.

On January 4, 1988, we commenced rehearsals. I was very pleased that John Lithgow had agreed to play the French diplomat, whom I named Rene Gallimard. Throughout his tenure with us, Lithgow was every inch the center of our company, intelligent and professional, passionate and generous. B. D. Wong was forced to endure a five-month audition period before we selected him to play Song Liling. Watching B.D.'s growth was one of the joys of the rehearsal process, as he constantly attained higher levels of performance. It became clear that we had been fortunate enough to put together a company with not only great talent, but also wonderful camaraderie.

As for Dexter, I have never worked with a director more respectful of text and bold in the uses of theatricality. On the first day of rehearsal, the actors were given movement and speech drills. Then Dexter asked that everyone not required at rehearsal leave the room. A week later, we returned for an amazingly thorough run-through. It was not until that day that I first heard my play read, a note I direct at many regional theatres who "develop" a script to death.

We opened in Washington, D.C., at the National Theatre, where *West Side Story* and *Amadeus* had premiered. On the morning after opening night, most of the reviews were glowing, except for *The Washington Post*. Throughout our run in Washington, Stuart never pressured us to make the play more "commercial" in reaction to that review. We all simply concluded that the gentleman was possibly insecure about his own sexual orientation and therefore found the play threatening. And we continued our work.

Once we opened in New York, the play found a life of its own. I suppose the most gratifying thing for me is that we had never compromised to be more "Broadway"; we simply did the work we thought best. That our endeavor should be rewarded to the degree it has is one of those all-too-rare instances when one's own perception and that of the world are in agreement.

Many people have subsequently asked me about the "ideas" behind the play. From our first preview in Washington, I have been pleased that people leaving the theatre were talking not only about the sexual, but also the political, issues raised by the work.

From my point of view, the "impossible" story of a French-man duped by a Chinese man masquerading as a woman always seemed perfectly explicable; given the degree of misunderstanding between men and women and also between East and West, it seemed inevitable that a mistake of this magnitude would one day take place.

Gay friends have told me of a derogatory term used in their community: "Rice Queen" —a gay Caucasian man primarily attracted to Asians. In these relationships, the Asian virtually always plays the role of the "woman"; the Rice Queen, culturally and sexually, is the "man." This pattern of relationships had become so codified that, until recently, it was considered unnatural for gay Asians to date one another. Such men would be taunted with a phrase which implied they were lesbians.

Similarly, heterosexual Asians have long been aware of "Yellow Fever"—Caucasian men with a fetish for exotic Oriental women. I have often heard it said that "Oriental women make the best wives." (Rarely is this heard from the mouths of Asian men, incidentally.) This mythology is exploited by the Oriental mail-order bride trade, which has flourished over the past decade. American men can now send away for catalogues of "obedient, domesticated" Asian women looking for husbands. Anyone who believes such stereotypes are a thing of the past need look no further than Manhattan cable television, which advertises call girls from "the exotic east, where men are king; obedient girls, trained in the art of pleasure."

In these appeals, we see issues of racism and sexism intersect. The catalogues and TV spots appeal to a strain in men that desires to reject Western women for what they have become—independent, assertive, self-possessed—in favor of a more reactionary model—the pre-feminist, domesticated geisha girl.

That the Oriental woman is penultimately feminine does not of course imply that she is always "good." For every Madonna there is a whore; for every lotus blossom there is also a dragon lady. In popular culture, "good" Asian women are those who serve the White protagonist in his battle against her own people, often sleeping with him in the process. Stallone's *Rambo II*, Cimino's *Year of the Dragon*, Clavell's *Shogun*, Van Lustbader's *The Ninja* are all familiar examples.

Now our considerations of race and sex intersect the issue of imperialism. For this formula—good natives serve Whites, bad natives rebel—is consistent with the mentality of colonialism. Because they are submissive and obedient, good natives of both sexes necessarily take on "feminine" characteristics in a colonialist world. Gunga Din's unfailing devotion to his British master, for instance, is not so far removed from Butterfly's slavish faith in Pinkerton.

It is reasonable to assume that influences and attitudes so pervasively displayed in popular culture might also influence our policymakers as they consider the world. The neo-Colonialist notion that good elements of a native society, like a good woman, desire submission to the masculine West speaks precisely to the heart of our foreign policy blunders in Asia and elsewhere.

For instance, Frances Fitzgerald wrote in *Fire in the Lake*, "The idea that the United States could not master the problems of a country as small and underdeveloped as Vietnam did not occur to Johnson as a possibility." Here, as in so many other cases, by dehumanizing the enemy, we dehumanize ourselves. We become the Rice Queens of *realpolitik*.

M. Butterfly has sometimes been regarded as an anti-American play, a diatribe against the stereotyping of the East by the West, of women by men. Quite to the contrary, I consider it a plea to all sides to cut through our respective layers of cultural and sexual misperception, to deal with one another truthfully for our mutual good, from the common and equal ground we share as human beings.

For the myths of the East, the myths of the West, the myths of men, and the myths of women—these have so saturated our consciousness that truthful contact between nations and lovers can only be the result of heroic effort. Those who prefer to by-pass the work involved will remain in a world of surfaces, misperceptions running rampant. This is, to me, the convenient world in which the French diplomat and the Chinese spy lived. This is why, after twenty years, he had learned nothing at all about his lover, not even the truth of his sex.

D. H. H.

New York City
September 1988